Gas Stations
COAST TO COAST

MICHAEL KARL WITZEL

MBI Publishing Company

Dedication

For Tine, may the hairball treat you well as you strive to maintain an orbit that you can live with. As you strive to maintain your equilibrium, keep watching for that baboon in the bush. He wants your banana, and will do everything he can to get it . . .

First published in 2000 by MBI Publishing Company, 729 Prospect Avenue, PO Box 1, Osceola, WI 54020-0001 USA

MBI Publishing Company books are also available at discounts in bulk quantity for industrial or sales-promotional use. For details write to Special Sales Manager at Motorbooks International Wholesalers & Distributors, 729 Prospect Avenue, PO Box 1, Osceola, WI 54020-0001 USA.

Library of Congress Cataloging-in-Publication Data available.

ISBN: 0-7603-0740-7

On the front cover:
There was a time when fueling your car meant service with a smile. This advertisement from the 1940s promotes Shell Oil Company's emphasized commitment to service by picturing a qualified service attendant. *Coolstock.com, courtesy of Shell Oil Company*

On the frontispiece:
All but entirely forgotten, license plate placards were once given away by many gasoline stations. Collected today due to rarity, these bits of "petroliana" stir feelings of nostalgia for the days of "full-service." *©2000 Coolstock.com*

On the title page:
Although its doors are closed for business, this clapboard gas station building evokes strong memories of small towns, full-service, and attendants. Today, the corporate superstation has taken over and muscled out the small-time filling station by shoving it into obscurity. *©2000 Coolstock.com*

On the back cover:
Top: The typical roadside gas station of the early days, complete with a Coca-Cola sign painted on the side of the building. Soda pop was one of the earliest roadside treats. *National Archives*

Center: Chrome and graffiti just seem to go together. The handwriting is on the wall, so to speak, and the generation of the gasoline station is nearing its close. The age of solar power is dawning and a new age of transportation is upon us. *©2000 Coolstock.com*

Bottom: A garage, gas station, and used car lot is a triple punch when it comes to marketing. Pick up an old jalopy, fill it up at the pumps, and drive it into the repair bay fix. These are the types of businesses that made America "Famous for Automobiles." *Courtesy Coolstock.com*

Endpapers:
This artwork was the backdrop for a Texaco dry-ethyl gasoline advertisement that ran in the *Saturday Evening Post* magazine during the 1920s. Back then, part of the filling station experience was service station attendants clad in jodhpurs and clockface gasoline pumps. *Coolstock.com Collection, Courtesy Texaco Inc.*

Edited by John Adams-Graf
Designed by Tom Heffron

Printed in China

Contents

Acknowledgments

A full-service, super-premium, wipe-the-windows-and-check-the-oil thank you goes out to all of the oil companies who assisted with material for this book, the photographers who supplied images, and the collectors who generously allowed me to use their precious petroliana heirlooms. Additional thanks is reserved for the real life gas station owners and attendants who lived it all and chose to freely share their time and memories. Of course, no gas station book acknowledgements page would be complete without mentioning Clare Patterson, Jr., the petroliana addict and lifelong collector who got me jump-started in this collectibles craze so long ago. As for the photo researchers and the creative team at Coolstock.com, your lifetime membership in the American Roadside Hall of Fame is secure, with unlimited mileage included. Thanks to all who participated in *Gas Stations Coast to Coast!*

Introduction

I always liked going to the gas station. Growing up during the 1960s, the American service station was a fun place to visit. For a kid who fantasized about automobiles and built intricate roadway systems in the backyard to run his collection of Matchbox, Corgi, and other toy cars, it was a magical place. This was the business that made cars go! This was where automobiles got their juice!

One year, I was lucky enough to get the electrified version of the Matchbox cars for Christmas and I vividly remember the plastic gasoline pump that came with the set. Attached to the tiny pumper was a plastic hosewell, which was actually a wire that plugged into the side of each little car to recharge the small battery inside. I really liked to run those babies and had to recharge those cars a lot. I learned early on that you can't get anywhere in something on wheels unless you have the means to replenish its power.

But there was more to the mystique of the neighborhood service station than just the idea of filling up a car with gasoline. It was a cool place filled with all of the wondrous machinery that performed all sorts of tasks and the men who knew how to make it all work. The gas station attendant dressed up in his full service regalia of bow tie and cap commanded a sense of awe and respect, like a man in the military or a police officer. He took command of his domain and made sure the job got done right, the first time. He was the backbone of the gas station.

Inside the station garage bay was a wonderland of tools and equipment, full-sized versions of the many toys that occupied my days of youth. What kid wasn't fascinated by the sight of a huge vehicle being hoisted up on a hydraulic lift? What red-blooded American child wouldn't have been thrilled to pull the lever that would heave the hulk high into the air, exposing its underbelly?

There was a lot of really neat stuff packed into the underside of a car and the distinctive whirring sound made by the pneumatic wrench as it spun-off wheel lugs or other bolts was a sound that really stuck in your mind. Equally memorable was the sight and sound of a tire being popped from the rim with one of those red Coates tire machines. With tools laying everywhere and guys covered in grease buried inside an engine compartment, it was a scene that branded itself into your brain. The gas station was a magical place.

Eventually, I came to learn the principles behind many of these strange devices and service procedures. As the years passed, the idealized vision of the gas station that I had as a child faded. Mind you, I still liked gas stations, it's just that I began taking them for granted like so many of us did before the services and values that we found there began to slide. Sadly, the gas station became just another business that I patronized—until something woke me from my slumber.

During the late 1970s, I began to notice that the stations I so adored during my younger days were changing. Station attendants didn't look as spiffy, full-service gas cost more, and garage service bays were difficult to find. Most of the time, getting gas meant operating the pump yourself at a self-service station. It was with a certain sadness that I noted and mourned the demise of the American filling station.

About that time, I picked up a camera and began photographing old gas stations and pumps, aware that the older, more striking models were disappearing. Fuel pumps were evolving into ugly chrome boxes. Convenience store stations echoed the blandness. Neon disappeared from the scene, replaced by fluorescent tubes. The spinning calculator wheels were electronic indicators, and the gas pump didn't ring at every gallon. My gas stations were gone.

By the end of the 1970s, the so-called "oil crisis" had left its mark on the roadside landscape and thousands of mom-and-pop filling stations were no more. As they went out of business, they took with them their old pumps, classic signs, and easy-going mode of business. The corporate superstation was on the rise. Big flashy cars were out, and small economy vehicles imported from Japan were in. Consuming large quantities of gas was as outmoded an idea as installing a four-barrel carburetor on a hot rod.

As this book goes to print, almost 20 years have gone by and history is once again repeating itself. The American gas station continues to undergo dramatic changes. Because of the supply and demand considerations of OPEC, prices for motor fuel and diesel have soared to an all-time high. In many regions of the country, some unlucky consumers are paying over $2 per gallon!

I guess nothing lasts forever, and that surely holds true for the friendly filling stations of days gone by. With all of the changes that have taken place through the years, the gas station is but a shadow of what it used to be. At least my memories can't be taken away! I'll *always* recall the friendly attendants who helped me put air into my bicycle tires, showed me how the car lift worked, and gave my parents advice on matters automotive.

—*Michael Karl Witzel*

Chapter 1

THE ROADSIDE SHOW CALLED GASOLIINE

ATTRACTING MOTORISTS TO THE PUMPS

When the gasoline station first appeared along the American roadside, it was a homely sight. From livery depots, bicycle repair shops, hardware emporiums, and drug stores, proprietors sold cans of gasoline to the few who required them. Early gas outlets were not even called "stations"—this term originally referred only to the gasoline pump and cabinet. Sellers of fuel were merely businesses that added gasoline to their inventories.

Before the automobile made its grand debut and stole the show from the horsedrawn carriage, demand was minimal and viewed as simply a byproduct of the oil refining process—a waste product. The main fuel source of the day was kerosene, a less volatile liquid that people used in lamps and stoves. Gasoline was occasionally used as a cleaning agent or as lamp fuel, often with explosive results.

While the automobile gained prominence as a mode of affordable and reliable transportation, gasoline assumed its rightful place. By 1910, kerosene was no longer such a hot commodity and it was gasoline that usurped its dominion. With more and more motorcars plying the trails and "roads," demand increased.

Greater demand meant that more businesses were selling gasoline. Instead of merely selling small amounts in tiny cans and containers, forward-thinking business owners maximized sales by positioning dedicated gas pumps on the street. Motorcar owners scanned the roadsides for a gas pump and when they saw one, they knew they were in luck. Out along Main Street, in front of the dry goods store, the post office, or the feed store stood curious pumping machinery that dispensed gasoline into the automobile tank.

In these formative days of fuel sales, vehicle owners and proprietors didn't express much preference among brands or types of gasoline. The horseless carriage was a new phenomenon and employing a generic designation to market fuel was considered an acceptable practice. After all, when trailblazers were stranded by an empty tank, finding combustible liquids was the predominant thought—regardless of the company that refined or distributed it. Individual brand preferences—like the loyalties that were established for soap flakes and cigarettes—weren't in place. As long as it had the same chemical properties and powered the internal combustion engine properly, it was good enough to go into the gas tank of an automobile. Besides, many of the nation's oil refiners were just getting started in this offshoot called gasoline sales. They invested heavily in the process of finding and refining oil and allocated scant resources to develop the markets. Consequently, they didn't reserve much of an ad budget when it came to the promotion of motoring products.

Eventually, the rising demand for gasoline spurred competition. If Clem's Hardware store on Main Street was vying for the same motorists as

The typical roadside gas station of the early days, complete with a Coca-Cola sign painted on the side of the building. Soda pop was one of the earliest roadside treats. *National Archives*

Sometimes the architecture of the station was used to pull in the traffic. The Painted Canyon station was made entirely of stones and created an imposing presence on the roadside. *Courtesy Coolstock.com*

Mayfield's Drugstore on Elm, both owners wanted a way to differentiate their gas from the other, even though each had the same fuel! The trick to pulling in trade was to have something better than the other vendor, and then to let the motoring public know about it. Thus was born the age of gas station hucksterism in America.

Gas oil refiners and station operators studied the power and techniques of advertising. At first, many took their cues from other successful ad campaigns. Why not employ the same tactics that cigarette and soda pop sellers of the era were using to sell their consumer goods? Why not give this foul-smelling liquid a more attractive name, infuse it with a little bit of personality, and begin plastering the roadsides with signs bearing the brand name? That was the way to sell gasoline!

By the 1920s, petroleum refiners (like the manufacturers of so many other consumer goods) began supplying its vendors with all kinds of signs. Emblazoned with a brand name or slogan,

these small and easy-to-mount signs could be easily attached to the side of a station or wall, near the pumps, or at a strategic point along the roads and byways. They were cost-effective to produce in large quantities and easy to ship to the dealers.

Generally known as "snipe" signs (because they called out to the consumer from almost every conceivable position), these small messages vied for attention. Usually, they were made of steel or pressed tin, and

White Horse Service Station, on Routes U.S. 20 and N.Y. 5, Irving, N. Y.   K5957

The White Horse station was not affiliated with Mobil's Flying Red Horse, but it still had unique drawing power. To get attention, the owners erected a replica of a horse on the roof and watched the cars roll in. *Courtesy Coolstock.com*

some were silk-screened with a special printing process. The colors were actually baked in, creating a porcelain-enamel finish the could withstand the elements of nature and the ravages of time. Along the American roadsides of the 1910s and 1920s, the snipe sign became a ubiquitous mode of advertising, evidenced by historical photographs of period businesses.

Eventually, there were just too many snipe signs for the consumer to digest, and gradually they lost their impact. Of course, this caused signmakers to fashion even larger signs, and station owners to develop new display methods. By the 1920s, it was common to see a large porcelain enameled sign raised high atop a tall sign pole or attached to the gable of a station hut. These placards were lit by electrically powered bulbs for customers arriving at night in

The first self-service, "serve-ur-self" gas station appeared in California, slowly changing the business of the gas station. In its own way, it attracted motorists to the pumps with the promise of low prices and fast fill-ups. ©2000 Mike Wallen, courtesy of Kent Bash

regions with electric service. Some refiners followed Mobil's lead and created circular signs that stood on a heavy cast-iron base, allowing proprietors to position them at the curbside and move them.

With that, the colorful streetside sign pole became the primary point of identification for the motorist—a common gas station element that persists to this day (although in radically different configurations and materials). For the car owner zooming along the highway, there was no confusion as to who sold gasoline.

By this time, the sale of gasoline was a thriving business and the major petroleum companies invested in even more elaborate types of signs. The age of the roadside billboard had begun.

To boost fuel sales during the 1920s, refiners such as Standard Oil Company installed immense signs in their wide sales regions. With a diameter of over 15 feet, the signs were larger than most other gasoline signs of the age. Scattered through the western region of the United States, these monstrosities promoted "Red Crown" gas as they gobbled up every inch of roadside scenery. The red and blue insignia branded its indelible image on the mind of the car owner. Before too long, motorists knew them as landmarks.

A similar gasoline-soaked image was branded on the brain of the magazine reader, too. As early as the 1910s, sellers of motor spirits found that the printed page was a cost-effective way to get the word out about their products. What better way to popularize a particular brand than to splash its qualities all over the pages of the public's favorite magazines? Standard, Socony, Sinclair, Shell, Texaco, Cities Service, Gulf, Atlantic, Tydol, Richfield, Sunoco, Conoco, Pure, Amoco, Gilmore, and Phillips—all of the established gasoline brands (and some lesser known independents) established a visible foothold in magazines.

Inspired by the "Sunflower State" nickname, Kanotex embossed the seed-rich flower of Kansas on its globes before the sunflower was adopted as part of the Kansas state flag in 1927. Originally Superior Refining, the Midwest oil enterprise trademarked its Kanotex name in 1909. Later, it began availing itself on one-piece etched globes to promote product. Although a few variations developed, these early globes featured a white star placed in front of a yellow sunflower bearing an oversized Kanotex "O." ©2000 Coolstock.com

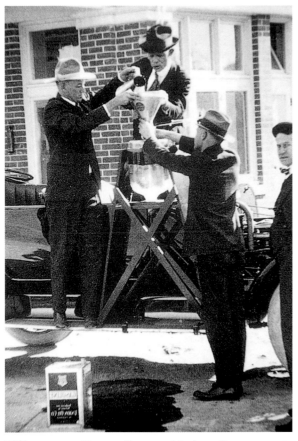

Filling a car with gasoline used to be a three person task. There were so many items required to do the job that an entire team was needed to do it right. *Courtesy the Arizona Historical Society*

The gas station and automotive showroom was at one time a potent combination for sales. First, sell them a car; then sell a tank of gasoline to run it. *Courtesy Coolstock.com*

The top media were widely read and admired publications such as the *Saturday Evening Post*, *American Magazine*, and *Life*. With oversized pages (compared to today's magazines) as large as 14x10-1/2 inches, these periodicals provided the perfect canvas for various combinations of images and text. While black and white was often used, full color played a big part in most gasoline ad campaigns and most advertisements were designed with lavish hues. Golden, glistening drops of oil issued forth from gleaming oil cans, station attendants waved toothy grins of welcome, and a myriad of animal mascots paraded their way across the printed page. These were the days before television, and Americans still liked to read—the ads simply came along for the ride.

However, printed advertising, snipe signs, illuminated metal signs, and oversized billboards fell short when compared to one single medium: neon. The

When automobiles were coming into their own, Gulf positioned grand stations, such as this Pennsylvania example, at busy street corners. The pumps alone were enough to make the motorist do a double-take. *Photograph provided, and reprinted with permission, by Chevron Corporation and its subsidiary, Chevron U.S.A. Inc.*

Mobilgas has always represented speed and power. This wartime ad depicts the Flying Red Horse in flight, promising to "put new life in your car!" Coolstock.com Collection, Courtesy Mobil Corporation

red, glowing tubes of neon officially debuted in the United States in 1923. That year, Los Angeles, California, automobile dealer Earle Anthony was "turned on" to the fragile creations produced by the Claude Neon Factory in Paris, France. Impressed by the vibrant glow of the energized tubes, he decided to exploit the new medium to sell motorcars.

Upon his return to America, he put his plan into action and slapped a pair of blue-bordered neon beauties high up on his auto dealership building. That very first night, passing cars jammed the boulevard to get a glimpse at the word "Packard" written out in searing orange tubing. No one—including the advertising men who worked at the downtown agencies—had seen anything like it before. The bold colors sent a shockwave through the industry as the days of the bulb-lit billboard and externally illuminated advertising sign were out of juice.

Seven years later, the patent to the non-corroding electrode expired, clearing the way for the mass-production of neon signs. Now, with the royalty issue moot, every sign shop in America was free to buy equipment and supplies and begin making them. It didn't take long for roadside businesses such as service stations to follow the lead of Mr. Anthony. By the end of the 1930s, a great majority of American gas stations, lubritoriums, and repair garages were festooned

In various configurations, the logos and trademarks of Socony, and later Mobil, capitalized on the popular color scheme of red, white, and blue. ©2000 Coolstock.com

with a kaleidoscope of electrified fun; however, neon wasn't the only attention-getting element at gas stations across America.

Using the same principles as the neon sign, the pump-mounted advertising globe stole its share of the show. Where neon tubing relied on the electrification of rare gases, gas pump globes took advantage of more conventional internal illumination. The globe became a colorful canvas for all manners of oil company trademarks, mascots, or logos and sang the praises of gasoline right there at the gas pump where the motorist could see them clearly.

Today's baby boomers store an extensive palette of images that recall the way it used to be at the corner filling station—perhaps Mobil's Flying Red Horse, the Texaco Star, or the streamlined fuselage of the airplane of Kanotex's "Aviation" fuel. For most of us who view the golden age of the gas station with fondness, the colorful gas pump globe often tops the list. Forty years ago—long before the advent of cheap, convenience store fuel—everyone had their favorite brand of gas and their favorite pump globe. Often, consumer loyalty was galvanized by the glowing ball of light atop the dispenser.

As it happened, the practice of mounting round billboards on top of gasoline dispensers began after

the first commercial pumps were perfected. To boost their sales, manufacturers like Tokheim and Gilbert & Barker inaugurated the globe tradition by crowning some of their early dial gauge units with glass balls. Just like the street lamp, the electrified globe lit the way for customers. Introduced by a number of

continued on page 20

Socony stations such as this Bethel, New York, example used to be common. Main Street was where American motorists first bought their gasoline and oil products. *Courtesy Coolstock.com*

The Co-op brand of gasoline was once a familiar sight in the Midwest. One can still see the logo today at grain mills and other agricultural operations. ©*2000 Coolstock.com*

Gasoline stations were spawned from the downtown business and grew from there. Busy intersections with a lot of traffic were the best place to situate such a service business, and the Spot Gasoline Drive-In took full advantage. *Courtesy Coolstock.com*

THE TOWER
OF TUCSON

Gas stations appear in almost every reel of film produced in Hollywood these days as the interest in nostalgia and America's yesteryear peaks. Since travel by automobile continues to play such a large part in personal transportation, it's difficult to avoid at least one visual reference to the gasoline station in the majority of motion pictures today.

With an endless amount of road-related themes including cross-country chase sequences, escapes from justice (and injustice), personal quests, and just plain traveling for fun, today's movie-goer is more likely to see a gas station pop up in the next flick showing at the local cinema than ever before.

When one of these eye-catching refueling stops appears on the big screen, it's usually the standard vision of what a classic gasoline station looked like. All the proper accessories and petroliana props are placed in just the right locations—including globe-topped gasoline pumps, porcelain-enameled signs, Coca-Cola coolers, and vintage vehicles. In the flickering sequence of pictures illuminated by a film projector, these idealized refueling scenes are maximized by the expert skills of professional directors, cinematographers, and experienced actors. Throw in a grizzled old station attendant played by an eccentric character actor and *voilà*: the perfect re-creation of a roadside refueling business comes to life.

Still, these brief glimpses of the homespun gasoline businesses that once proliferated along Americas highways are sometimes just clever illusions, carefully crafted for the camera lens to appear true-to-life when projected on the silver screen, when they are often only forgotten buildings decaying at the fringes of once-thriving communities.

In many cases, they are only dusty spots on the sides of remote highways way out West, chosen for their overall view and effect.

Location scouts contracted by the major film production companies make it their jobs to routinely scour the little-known backroads of America, searching for suitable filming locations and abandoned buildings that may be remade to resemble the film director's vision. When just the right setting is found, prop departments and set designers coordinate their efforts to secure the necessary gas station equipment and signs. They quickly restore and re-create the gasoline alleys of yesteryear—just long enough to film the scenes dictated by the script.

When a suitable building cannot be located, an entire building façade must be constructed from scratch and meticulously modeled after historical photographs and archival images. Whether created in the studio or on location, the stations created tend to have more visual appeal than their authentic counterparts.

For the Tucson Tower in Arizona, that axiom proved false. It already possessed all of the visual appeal a gas station could hope for when Columbia pictures chose it as a filming location in the early 1980s for their movie *Stir Crazy*. It only needed a few refinements to bring it up to true star level.

It took only a few short days for set crews to upgrade the adobe structure. The large tubular turret, finned like the lower stage of a Jules Verne rocket ship, received a fresh coat of paint along with the rest of the surfaces comprising the interesting art-deco design. To accent the trio of decorative "speed lines" on the canopy, the drive-thru was recoated with color. Meanwhile, workmen mounted an eye-catching Union 76 sign on the top side of the large overhang.

Gas stations appear in almost every reel of film produced in Hollywood these days. Sometimes, the glimpse of the gasoline business is just a clever illusion. The Tower of Tucson was one such fuel stop, making its screen debut in the movie *Stir Crazy*. ©2000 Coolstock.com

Every detail was taken care of as lights, sound equipment, and cameras were readied for action. Director Sydney Poitier gave the word for Gene Wilder and Richard Pryor to exchange their lines under the canopy while the attendant in the scene collected their cash. After a few takes and various camera angles, the short segment was in the bag. Almost a week's worth of work and preparation were over. The production crew had what they wanted, now recorded on undeveloped reels of film stock.

Piece by piece, the entourage dismantled their equipment and removed the signs and accessories that had briefly invigorated the station with new life. Within hours, Tucson's unique tower station had reverted back to its former identity. Today, it is business as usual as Lupita Shestko-Montiel runs her 24-hour bail-bond service from the space once occupied by service bays, while an attorney handles cases from an office under the turret.

So the next time you are settled into a seat at the local movie house and spy a scene featuring a gas station, don't get too excited about trying to find its location. It probably doesn't even exist in the real world. More likely, it's a total fabrication born of an art director's fertile imagination. But it doesn't really matter—for the majority of Americans who hold a special fondness for old-time service stations, a movie ticket will continue to be their passport to visit the classics.

Phillips 66 Flite fuel was advertised by means of shield-shaped globes positioned on the tops of gas pumps. If you didn't have a neon sign or billboard, the gas pump globe was the next best thing for attracting the business. © _Coolstock.com_

Continued from page 15

pump makers in 1912, these all-in-one globes were cast in a mold with an opaque, milky-white glass.

Initially, the Wayne Pump Company rolled out a simple one-piece globe to finish out their Cut 276 model gas pump. However, flashy advertising was not this beacon's mission. Primarily, its function was to identify its host as a gasoline pump. Perched atop a tall post where car customers passing by could see it, the glowing gas pump globe lent respectability to what otherwise was a rather unattractive machine—especially after sunset.

At the time, the majority of representations made by these unpretentious orbs were accomplished with generalities: "Filtered Gasolene" [sic] was one of the first globe terms to be used. Quickly, it became widely accepted as the standard inscription. At first, the words were painted, then permanently etched into heavy glass. Most manufacturers of the early pump era bundled similar globes with their dispensers, constraining details to basic description.

Gradually, restrained variations on this "all-round" globe theme were made. From this basic configuration, the one-piece glass sub-classifications known as etched, raised-letter, baked-on (or fired-on), and sculptural globes were developed. Today, with prices ranging from a low of $500 to $850 and sometimes more, all of these early one-piece globe styles are prominent in the current globe hobby and are widely traded by today's collectors in a field commonly referred to as "petroliana."

To insure the durability and weather-resistance of the lettering inscribed upon them, the glass surfaces of the first etched globes were carved in all of the areas where paint was to be applied. After color filled the rough surfaces (usually red) and dried, it bonded onto the glass. It was a simple way to make a gas pump globe without securing the skills of a skilled painter. But this unadorned style didn't come to rule the domain of globes. With increased competition in the retail sales market, many oil refiners decided to differentiate their distillations even more. To preserve their share of the consumer's dollar and keep it, refining companies debuted custom pump globes depicting individually named, unique brands of gasoline. The simple words of description fell quickly to elaborate scenes and slogans.

With the debut of colorful graphics, stylized typography, engaging mascots, and bold insignias,

Before the age of plastic, oil was distributed in cans. Brands such as Roadrunner captured the imaginations of consumers, and in turn, influenced them to buy their brand of oil. ©*2000 Coolstock.com*

It's ironic that most of the oil, gas, and other petroleum distillates were delivered by horse power during the early decades of refining. *From the Collections of Henry Ford Museum & Greenfield Village*

Defiance

REG. **U.S. PAT. OFF.**

The
SPARK PLUGS
of
**Predetermined
Quality**
•

Defiance Spark Plugs, Inc., Toledo, Ohio

To all who sell and to all who use spark plugs . . . Defiance offers spark plugs of predetermined quality . . . and also an exceptional spark plug service by direct Defiance field representatives. . . The unique Defiance Merchandising Plan is, today, especially favorable both to those who are interested in profits from the sale of automotive necessities and to those wishing to reduce the investment in spark plug stocks required in servicing their own fleets.

The service station attendant did more than pump gas. The attendant was also responsible for station sales, and sparkplugs were just one small piece of the marketing puzzle. *Coolstock.com Collection*

once unbranded "gasoline" transcended from a generic commodity into a liquid that had verve and vitality. At the hands of America's gifted advertising men, motor fuels assumed a myriad of memorable personalities. Later, the gasoline refiners that produced such brand names as Red Crown, Pennzoil, White Rose, Purol, and others heightened the stakes when they started implementing splashier letter fonts and logos. By the end of the 1920s, the once globular pump ball was transformed, becoming more like a flattened doughnut without a hole. Raised lettering, cast relief, specialized glass effects, and stylized body configurations were the icing.

As petroleum companies jumped on the bandwagon of brand identity and began applying distinct identities to their fuel, the pump globe became a miniature billboard to display images. Before too long, a palette of stylized trademarks were applied

onto the glass of the pump globe. Whether painted on or silk-screened, gasoline pump globes featured colorful renditions of airplanes, eagles, and Indian chiefs. To effect permanence and resistance to the elements, the paint was baked on or fired right into the glass.

When combined with raised lettering, etched glass, and other features, globes were on their way to becoming miniature works of art. Today, pristine examples of these fired-on gas pump globes command some of the loftiest prices in the hobby. Especially beautiful one-piece picture globes have recently zoomed into the substantial range of $2,000 to $5,000!

As the technology for casting glass and the techniques for decoration improved, the sheer variety of gasoline pump globes exploded. Suddenly, the idea of adorning a pump with words alone was no longer enough. At the request of a few companies, molders experimented with exotic designs. Pump-mounted beacons that featured three-dimensional features were on their way.

To characterize their motor fuel, the White Eagle division of Socony-Vacuum Oil capitalized on the patriotic connections that were rooted in national pride. By using the majestic shape of an eagle for their gas pump globe, they conjured up feelings of patriotism and strength at the gas pump. At filling stations located throughout Kansas and the Midwest, internally illuminated eagles pulled in the customers and kept a watchful eye on the thriving business of refueling automobiles.

But the Socony White Eagles were not the only attractive globes in town. A number of oil companies debuted one-piece globes cast of molded glass. Most memorable today is the Shell Oil Company clamshell-shaped globe, a pump-top beauty that reinforced the Shell corporate name with particular aplomb (this globe is highly prized in petroliana collecting circles). Cities Service followed a close second with their clever clover-shaped models sporting raised letters. Of course, who can forget the Phillips 66 brand and the highway shield–shaped globe?

With all of these visual elements in place, the refined gasoline products that had once been perceived

The service station ashtray was a premium giveaway that got plenty of use. Back during the days when smoking was chic, it was all the rage to have an ashtray from your favorite gas station. ©2000 Coolstock.com

During the early decades of gasoline sales, oil was dispensed in beautiful glass containers. ©2000 Coolstock.com

This scene from the General Petroleum Museum in Seattle, Washington, depicts much of the ambience found at America's first gas stations. *©2000 Coolstock.com, courtesy the General Petroleum Museum*

In 1931, Shell produced a series of well illustrated maps. This example illustrates the age old act of stopping the car and asking the locals for directions. *Coolstock.com Collection, courtesy Shell Oil Company*

In this impersonal age of high-speed interstate highways and homogenized roadside franchises, finding a gas station with small-town style and ethical service values is becoming increasingly difficult. Like this Enumclaw, Washington, refueler, most of the stations with any sort of character are far from the convenience of the freeway off ramp. ©2000 Coolstock.com

FLYING THE RED HORSE

Mobil's dauntless mascot, the Pegasus, commands attention everywhere it's seen. Whether it's making its way into the sky on a hot trail of neon or affixed to a station building in the form of pressed steel, it's been a familiar brush stroke on the roadside canvas for more than 50 years. There has never been another petro-company trademark like it, and there will never be again.

According to the Mobil Oil Corporation, the venerable Flying Red Horse was adopted as a logo in the United States shortly after the merger of the Standard Oil Company of New York and Vacuum Oil in 1931. Prior to that, Vacuum had employed a gargoyle to identify its lubrication products. However, after the corporate union, a new identity was needed to represent joint products. For the modern market of gasoline consumers, a majestic steed was deemed the perfect choice to symbolize the idea of speed and power.

Nevertheless, some gasoline historians report that the Pegasus made its first showing in 1911. That year, a Mobil predecessor in South Africa employed a white, artful rendition of the winged equine to identify its refined goods. The image was used by many refineries and although rare, can still be seen at some of the older refineries. A recent example was rescued from the Mobil refinery in Augusta, Kansas, and is now part of the display at the White Eagle Antique mall on the outskirts of town.

The airborne animal didn't remain colorless for long. It's said that the Mobil Sekiyu division in Japan first colored the four-footed creature red. This wasn't to be the end of the horse's visual makeover: During the 1930s, cowboy artist (and commercial illustrator) Robert "Rex" Elmer revamped the horse, creating a more idealized version. The naive outline of the early configuration was dropped and illustrative strokes added. Further definition of the head, wings, mane, and tail resulted from the overall reversal of the image.

Throughout the following decades, the flying mascot continued its gradual metamorphosis. In 1954, the basic design received a graphic facelift when the white lines were thinned a little bit—lending a subtle hint of streamlined sophistication to the logo. A more dramatic new direction was taken in 1965 when the entire beast reared up and flipped to the right, no doubt a direct result of McCarthyism and the "red scare" of the 1950s. Now, the horse was flying in the right direction! At the same time, the fanciful curves seen in the original red horse were reduced to their most elemental form.

In 1966, Socony Mobil Oil Company celebrated its 100th anniversary and changed its name to Mobil Oil Corporation. All around the world, the company updated its service stations to reflect a new sense of modernism. That year, well known architect and industrial designer Elliot Noyes worked with Mobil marketers and advertisers to develop a unique service station design. This new, minimalist station would become the standard for Mobil outlets worldwide. Mobil wanted this new design to be a radical departure from the days of old, yet still allow for the remodeling of old stations and the construction of new ones.

The bold result was the "Pegasus Station," an advanced refueling depot that equaled the visual panache of Detroit's latest automobiles. The Pegasus station featured an uncluttered design with distinctive circular canopies, cylindrical gasoline pumps (that looked like friendly robots), and a low-profile service building constructed entirely of brick and glass.

In terms of customer appeal and recognition, there will never be another trademark like Mobil's Flying Red Horse. Adorned in bright red neon, Peggy remains the most captivating trademark. ©2000 Coolstock.com, Courtesy the General Petroleum Museum

As for the signage, the less-is-more idea prevailed. Now, the graphic trotter that once held a position of prominence was set in a circular field of white. Emblazoned on an internally illuminated plastic disc, the tireless mascot was corralled on the side of the station wall. The word "Mobil," represented by a signature red "O" and thick blue lettering, emerged as the dominant theme on the station sign pole. While it survived the Noyes redesign, the Flying Red Horse had been demoted.

Fortunately, Mobil saw the wisdom in keeping the Flying Red Horse around, albeit in a less prominent form. Motorists the world over had come to know and love Peggy and there's no doubt that eliminating her completely would have caused outrage.

Today, petroliana collectors around the globe are obsessed with all sorts of collectibles featuring the Flying Red Horse. Whether it's porcelain-enameled or neon signs, gasoline pump placards, calendars, oil containers, gas pump globes, bug spray, postcards, or other trinkets, objects that depict the image of the Socony or Mobil Pegasus continue to be in great demand, and why not? The gallant red steed endures to this day, still adept at capturing the imagination of consumers. In the same class as Coca-Cola's logo, Mr. Peanut, and the Marlboro man, she flies to glory along the roadsides. Look, up in the sky—it's a bird, it's a plane, it's a flying red horse!

Main Street gas stations did little to pull in the crowds. All that was necessary in this high-traffic location was a streetside sign and some gas pumps.
Courtesy Coolstock.com

Reminiscent of the wayside inn or country tavern, the Modern Restaurant appears to have begun its life as a house. More than likely, pumps were added later to attract more tourists and highway trade moving down Route 22.
Courtesy Coolstock.com

Located in Avon, Connecticut, the Avon Diner had quite a roadside business going. In addition to the rental of small overnight cabins out back, they pumped gasoline of various brands. During the 1920s, it was common to see more than one brand being sold at a roadside refueling station. *Courtesy Coolstock.com*

AVON DINER — AVON, CONN. — J. W. ANDERSON, PROP.   2A-H463

The Socony Pegasus was an image that branded itself in the minds of motorists, which caused them to remember the brand when it was time to refuel the family car. *©2000 Coolstock.com*

Continued from page 28

maximum contest promotion. To help treasure-seekers with their search, mysterious "clew slips" were passed out to enthusiastic motorists who were interested in joining the upcoming festivities. Station buildings were adorned with the skull and cross-bones of the Jolly Roger. The words "Pirate Treasure Hunt" were emblazoned in paint, across the roof. A treasure chest display took a place of prominence atop the roof as attendants dressed in full pirate regalia pumped the gas.

Meanwhile, many of the other petroleum refineries ventured into the mass marketing arena. The Skelly Oil Company was one of the leaders when they launched a radio and newspaper ad campaign in 1925. This was no ordinary promotion, as company officials had the goal of "making the Skelly name a household word." To make this happen, their first broadcast went over the airwaves on a radio station in Tulsa, Oklahoma. Later, the company went coast-to-coast with a nationwide format. *The Skelly Hour* was a 30-minute broadcast that originated from the NBC studios in Chicago.

Featured in the program were entertainers such as Marian West, the "Skelly Smile Girl," with a 24-man chorus called the "Skellodians." Copying some of the other popular radio shows of the day, Skelly also had two characters by the names of "Tag and Lene," a pair of black-faced comedians (a take-off on the Amos and Andy show). Named after one of Skelly's motor oil brand names, this slapstick duo captured the attention of listeners—in spite of its ethnic insensitivity.

In those days, the content of the programming itself didn't really matter that much. Like the motor-car was during its early days, radio was a novelty. Just the fact that one could get any type of entertainment through the air was considered a miracle. For this reason, audiences were quite receptive to commercial advertising and promotion. Unjaded, they took it all in with open ears. It's curious to note that Skelly

The old and the new meet at this wayside service station for repairs and gasoline. Amoco stations, such as this example, used to house garage bays for service work. *National Archives*

Gasoline pump globes, such as this Vickers brand model, played on the idea of internal illumination. When it came to pulling in motorists off the streets, there was nothing like the glow of a friendly globe in the dark of night. ©2000 Coolstock.com

received a lot of fan mail from the listening audience, with little commentary about the content of the show or the commercials. The majority of the listeners wrote in about the clarity of their reception!

Radio continued to be a driving force in the marketing of motor fuel and oils throughout the 1930s. At the same time, the Pure Oil Company took to the airwaves with the sounds of Vincent Lopez and his Pure Oil Orchestra. Later, Pure was a proud sponsor for H.V. Kaltenborn on the NBC Radio Network. As competition from television increased during the 1950s, they produced a quiz show program called *Who Said That?* and broadcast it live over the 16-station NBC network. It was all part of the grand scheme to sell gallons of gasoline, and of course, pound home the slogan "Be Sure With Pure" into the minds of the consumer.

With about 40,000 filling stations spread nationwide, Texaco jumped on the advertising juggernaut

Rows and rows of gas pumps greeted the motorist at the gas stations of yesteryear. Today, individual units have given way to three-in-one machines with little character. ©2000 Coolstock.com

Sinclair was one of the early oil companies in the game. "Dino the Dinosaur" was one of their most popular mascots, and Dino graced signs and gas pumps everywhere. Motorists liked the imagery and flocked to the gas pumps to refuel their cars. ©2000 Coolstock.com

Tire inflators, like this Eco unit, offered air for free, unlike many of the pay-as-you-pump air hoses found at the modern supermarket gas station. ©2000 Coolstock.com

and made the broadcasting medium their own. When they introduced their new Fire Chief gasoline in 1933, they tied the brand to comedian Ed Wynn by sponsoring his radio program. On Tuesday nights, Texaco Fire Chief Wynn took to the airwaves following the sounds of the siren and bell. Announcer Graham McNamee played straight man as Wynn made merry, opening with "Ladies and gentlemen, on behalf of the Texaco Company—and I'd like to be half of the Texaco Company . . ."

The program was a major hit and was cross-promoted with full-page ads in the *Saturday Evening Post*. Texaco even made a die-cut mask of Wynn's face and fireman hat, an item that was snapped up by kids at the gas stations. By the time the show ended in 1935, an audience of more than one million listeners was tuning in regularly. As the program tag line said: "Tune in your radio again each Tuesday night and when you hear the sound of the siren and bell, think of Texaco Fire Chief gasoline. The finest gasoline we've ever made!" Because of radio, Texaco was on a roll and the revenues were pouring in faster than ever before.

But radio was small potatoes when compared to the attention gained by the new advertising and entertainment medium known as television. During the late 1940s, Texaco continued to lead the way with an offering they called the *Texaco Star Theater*, a television program that featured an up-and-coming entertainer by the name of Milton Berle (later known by all as Uncle Miltie).

During the opening of the show, a singing quartet of Texaco gas station attendants introduced the cigar-smoking comic with a rousing rendition of the Texaco theme song. In full uniform and set against a painted backdrop depicting a modern Texaco station, each of the four sang a particular verse of the song, depending on his job task. The first man held a pump nozzle, the second a wrench, the third a polishing cloth and hubcap, and

the fourth a small jack. It was all in great fun, and quite memorable, as a quartet of overexuberant gas station attendants yodeled, "Oh, we're the men of Texaco, we work from Maine to Mexico. There's nothing like this Texaco of ours, our show tonight is powerful. We'll wow you with an hour-full, of howls from a showerful of stars. We're the Merry Texaco men. Tonight we may be show men, tomorrow we'll be servicing your cars!"

With successful programs like the *Texaco Star Theater*, the 1950s radio advertising climate became competitive. Television shoved radio "out of the picture" and gasoline stations needed something exciting to lure customers to the pumps. And with that began the era off gimmicks and games. Gas station idea men dreamed up every conceivable idea under the sun in

The sight glass, resembling a small eye on the top of this vintage pump, allowed the motorist to see the gasoline that was flowing into the vehicle's gas tank. ©2000 Coolstock.com

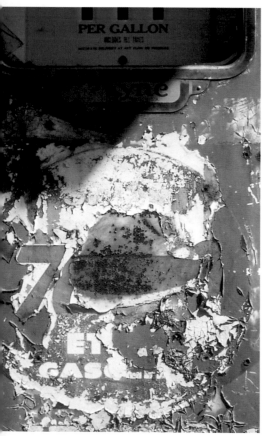

The only thing that remains constant in the business of gasoline sales is change. This peeling, retired gasoline pumper was found outside of Seattle, Washington. ©2000 Coolstock.com

order to interest people's imaginations and cause them to buy. Before it was all said and done, service stations of all brands were giving away everything from stamps to mink coats to Cadillacs.

By 1955, America's gas stations were spending big bucks on all of this flashy promotion. It was estimated by publications such as *National Petroleum News* that the industry was spending $42 million a year. By the late 1960s, big players in the trade were plunking down an amazing $150 million on trading stamps alone, and still another $100 million was lavished on game pieces and prizes.

The marketing frenzy reached its peak in 1965 when the Tidewater Oil Company produced a promotion they called "Win-a-Check." By matching game pieces given away at the company gas stations, excited motorists could win big cash prizes and

continued on page 41

1891

First Wayne Product - Kerosene Dispenser
U.S. patent 473,891

In 1891, the first gas pump, manufactured by Wayne Pump Company, was housed in a wooden cabinet.
Courtesy the Wayne Pump Company

The Bowser "Red Sentry" was one of the earliest "blind" gas pumps used commercially. Its dial indicator read gallons sold and could be rigged to give false readings. ©2000 Coolstock.com

THE FLYING RED HORSE LADY

Billie Butler really loves red horses. She has a small herd corralled out in her backyard and a few of them tied up in the living room. Some of them are large, while others are small enough to occupy a place of prominence on top of a cabinet in her dining room. Two of her special favorites stand watch 24 hours a day just behind the television in her den.

To the uninitiated, it might seem as if Mrs. Butler is in violation of local zoning ordinances and livestock laws, but that couldn't be farther from the truth. Her horses never need to be watered or curried, and mucking out a stable has never been one of her chores. After all, the horses that share her small suburban home in Augusta, Kansas, are simply a collection of advertising for the Mobil Oil Corporation.

Butler started collecting the Flying Red Horse memorabilia many years ago and has grown to love the striking symbol of speed and power. The airworthy "Peggy" is now an extended part of her family. It all started with her husband: For more than 38 years, Bob Butler was employed as a professional construction supervisor for the White Eagle oil concern (a subsidiary of SOCONY), working beneath the reassuring wings of the gallant red steed.

Upon retirement from the company in 1983, Bob left specific instructions with his associates to keep an eye out for available red horses. His name went on the list for the Pegasus sign that was to be removed from the main gate of the big Augusta refinery. During the late 1990s, the petroleum distillery was scheduled for demolition and souvenirs were reserved. Eventually, the Butlers won custody of one large, porcelain-enameled Pegasus sign.

Within a few short years, the Butler's impressive inventory of Mobil mascots garnered its share of publicity far beyond the Augusta borders. A number of antique magazines printed articles about the collection and newspapers picked up on the story. All of this hoopla happened long before collectors began hoarding gas station artifacts. It was a unique hobby, and Mobil's company newsletter even featured the acquisitive Butlers in one of their issues, introducing current employees to "petroliana."

The high point of the Butler's collecting craze came during the late 1990s when Billie's equine goods caught the attention of the *Star*, a national tabloid. An eager editor interviewed her by phone as a team of photographers swooped down from Kansas City to photograph her collection. When her issue hit the checkout lines, she became a minor celebrity. Butler grabbed hold of her 15 minutes of fame and enjoyed every minute of the ride.

Fortunately, she's come down from the clouds since then. For years she continued to check her mailbox to see "just what else someone may have sent her." Since the article's debut, packages and letters flowed in from all over North America. Surprisingly, many of the parcels contained sought after gas station goods for her expanding collection. Although a few came addressed to "The Flying Red Horse Lady," they all managed to get delivered.

The most notable donation came from a former Mobil worker living in New York. He owned a metal prototype of the 48-inch Pegasus button planned for use at stations redesigned by architect Elliot Noyes during the late 1960s. Ready for immediate shipment to the excited Mrs. Butler, he offered her the prized artifact for just the cost of one-way

Billie Butler, the Flying Red Horse Lady of Augusta, Kansas, poses with one of her favorite Mobil Pumps. Her husband worked at the local oil refinery for years, and when he retired, Butler acquired a penchant for collecting. ©2000 Coolstock.com

freight. Since an acrylic plastic version of the sign was ultimately used by Mobil, Billie knew the metal disc was a priceless gasoline treasure.

As the years passed, Billie learned what most collectors eventually learn: objects are never yours forever. Even for a collector, they are just "on loan" until they pass into the hands of another person. And so, as the passage of time changed Billie and small-town Augusta, she turned her attentions toward other priorities. She had reveled in the enjoyment of her cherished artifacts for many years and felt it was time to pass them on.

Because it was such a unique assortment of goods, she made a decision that the collection would have to be sold off as one unit—kit and caboodle. Of course the word spread like wildfire on the gasoline collecting circuit. A major petroliana buff got wind of the news and wasted no time making a respectable offer. On the day of the sale, a collection that took years to acquire was loaded into a big semi-trailer within a matter of hours.

Billie Butler's flying red horse collection was gone, but her reputation remained intact. Every once in a while, people still send her Flying Red Horse stuff in the mail and make her day. Her legend endures. And that's a good thing, because in these parts, she will always be known as the Flying Red Horse Lady.

Continued from page 37

become "instant winners." The public loved the roadside lottery, and for a time, they couldn't get enough of it. At Tidewater stations in California, gasoline sales shot up 56.5 percent in one month! Of course, the competition was watching. By the next year, everyone jumped into the fray and the American roadsides were bursting with gas station contests of every description. It was as if Las Vegas had moved from the Nevada strip to all the gas pump islands of America—the only thing missing was a fuel dispenser with a slot machine built right in (interestingly enough, a pump using this payoff principle would appear in later decades).

Independent stations and oil producers were forced to follow the crowd, and many came out with promotional games of their own. Many fuel sellers were reluctant to play this game of follow the leader, but felt like they had to participate in order to remain competitive. As the friction heated things up, a minority of customers began complaining about certain contests. Who was winning all of this money? Were all of the prizes given away? As these questions sought answers, the handwriting appeared on the gas station wall. It was just a matter of time before the empire built on crazy giveaways and prizes came tumbling down.

As the 1960s ended, an examining eye was turned onto the games and gimmicks. Governmental authorities began to make threatening gestures at the contests and started questioning their fairness. To curb what they called "widespread" unfair and deceptive gas station practices, the Federal Trade Commission proposed two important gaming rules that they wanted the stations to follow. Refiners cringed at the thought of this curbside regulation.

The first rule called for prohibiting the "rigging" of games and misrepresenting the chances of winning. If the odds of a poor Joe winning were one in a billion, it was expected that the station advertise that fact. In regards to games of chance, the second edict prohibited companies from coercing retail dealers to join in. Naturally, the majors denied that they were forcing participation. Official hearings were on the horizon.

Yes, the unpretentious era of gasoline advertising had lost its innocence. The hubris of big oil companies turned the marketing of motor fuel into a carnival that caught the fancy of every American car owner. Millions of motorists gladly paid to see the show and peered over the dashboard to see what would come next.

The history of petroleum marketing is filled with countless stories of filling stations that were born, lived, and died. Along the roadsides of America, progress takes many casualties. ©2000 Coolstock.com

Chapter 2

FILL'ER TO THE TOP WITH ETHYL GAS

A WORLD OF SERVICE AT THE GAS PUMP

Motorists seldom pondered the significance of the whirring, clanging, gasoline machine that pumped fuel into the family flivver. At the neighborhood filling station, it was viewed as an ordinary utility—not much to be excited about. After all, the act of pumping gas was less than glamorous: when a car pulled up for a refill, the service station attendant shoved a dripping nozzle into the filler neck and turned a crank, pumped a lever, or switched on a motor. Fuel surged through a flexible filler hose and into the tank. One of three methods was used to measure quantity: an indicator scale measured the liquid in a large crucible, a timepiece tallied top-off with a clock dial, or a revolving set of wheels calculated the dispensed amount in gallons.

Inside their automobiles, the customers would wait and gaze out of their windows. Eager to return to the frenzy of traffic, vehicle owners were largely ignorant of the gasoline pump's innovation and how it had become what it was. What really concerned customers the most was the current price per gallon, whether their premium cards were punched, and how clean their windshields were.

Not surprisingly, no one seemed to notice when the artful embellishments that infused the "ordinary" gasoline dispenser with personality were dropped. No one squawked when illuminated advertising globes were eliminated. By the time the fuel dispenser had evolved into a squat, chrome-plated monolith, memories of the once-friendly filling attendant had already faded. The fuel pump had gone high-tech.

But the history and evolution of the gasoline pump is a tale of engineering pluck and know-how that began more than 100 years ago with Sylvanus F. Bowser. It was 1895—ages before automobiles ruled the roads—when Mr. Bowser inaugurated the fledgling business of selling gasoline with the invention of America's first practical fuel dispenser.

Designed to pump coal oil for lamps, stoves, and heaters, his prototype was fashioned from an oil barrel and fitted with a wooden plunger on the center of the top side. With marbles serving as valves, it functioned like a water pump: a small piston attached to a hand-actuated lever created the vacuum to draw liquid from the tank. As gasoline moved from the status of waste product to one that was in great demand, Bowser continued his experimentation. In 1905, he unveiled an improved model suitable for pumping both kerosene and gasoline. His "Bowser Self-Measuring Gasoline Storage Pump" consisted of a 50-gallon metal tank enclosed within a weather-resistant storage cabinet made of wood, and a pumping device that featured pre-determined quantity-stops and fume vents. By moving a forced-suction plunger with a hand-stroke lever, an operator could dispense gas to automobiles with a flexible hose. It was such a great gadget that enthusiastic company salesman Jake Gumpper dubbed it a "filling station."

The curbside gas pump was once a common sight in towns across the nation. However, they were a fire hazard because cars often smashed into them, and in turn, many municipalities banned their use. *National Archives*

This Streamline Moderne Mobil station subscribed to the "flow" philosophy of pumping gas. All pump islands are strategically located to enable cars to pull in and out of the station with a minimum of hassle. *Courtesy Coolstock.com*

NORTHLAND MOTORS, INC.
LAKE PLACID GARAGE
Lake Placid, N. Y.

ROY STAUFFER CHEVROLET
801 - 805 Wyoming Avenue, West Pittston, Pa.

Car dealerships often sold gasoline to fill the tanks of their new cars, and those of passing customers. While motorists waited at the pumps, they gazed into the showroom window and dreamed. It was a great layout for new car sales. *Courtesy Coolstock.com*

During the era of visible-register pumps, a few of America's petroleum refiners got the notion to color their gasoline. To add personality to an otherwise unexciting liquid, dye was added to ordinary motor fuel according to its grade. An amber color signified "regular" gasoline, or the cheapest grade sold. A red or blue coloring identified "premium" gas. A clear, colorless gasoline was often reserved for utility fuels sold to farmers.

Many refiners tried the gimmick. Out on the West Coast, an independent doing business as the Gilmore Oil Company sold "Blu-Green" gasoline from its visible pumps (famous for its "Roar With Gilmore" slogan). Before too long, station-goers even came to know the brand by the color of the gas: Texaco featured a green gasoline, Sunoco blue, and Esso red! By the end of the decade, motorists could identify brand and grade from the front seat!

But colored gasoline was a short-lived fad. Petroleum refiners had other tricks up their sleeve, most notable being the use of grandiose architecture. As early as 1922, *The American City* magazine featured a rather unusual gasoline station that included classical Greek architecture. Instead of the usual pump island

BOB DUCHANO'S SANBORNVILLE GARAGE

"Famous for Automobiles"

SANBORNVILLE GARAGE

At Junction of Routes 16 & 109

In The Village of Sanbornville, N.H.

90423

A used car lot, gas station, and garage is a triple punch when it comes to marketing. Pick up an old jalopy, fill it up at the pumps, and drive it into the repair bay to get it running properly. These are the types of businesses that made America "Famous for Automobiles." *Courtesy Coolstock.com*

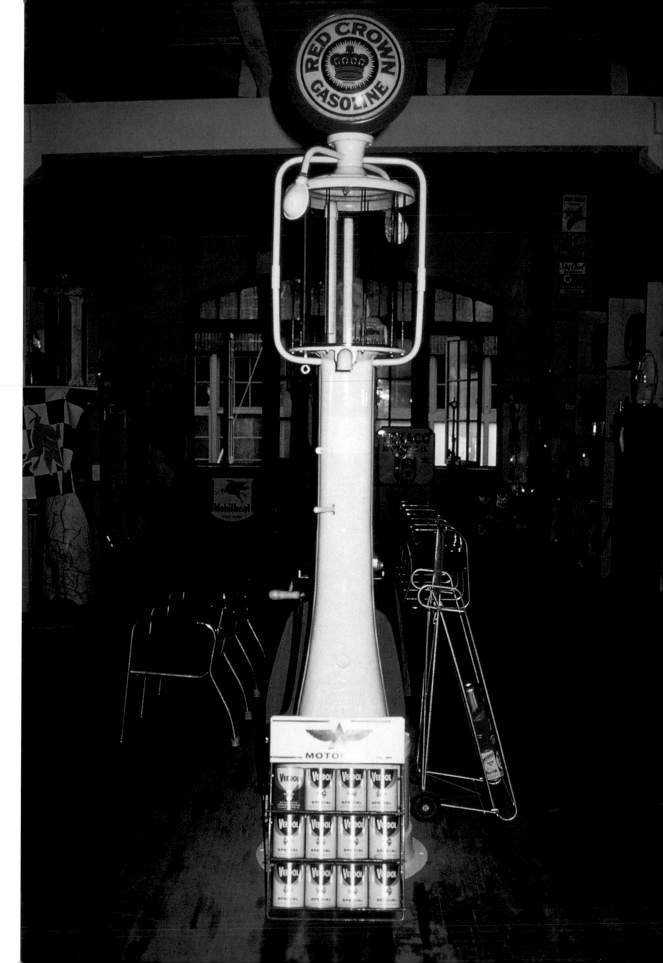

This Tokheim Cut No. 700 gas pump employed a clockface style of metering. The clockface was a major improvement over the simple blind pumps, but it still did not offer the motorist a chance to see the gas flowing into the tank. *Courtesy Tokheim Corporation*

The so-called "Mae West" visible register gas pump, named for its shapely curves, was a common sight at the gas stations of the 1920s. The glass crucible at the top of the pump allowed customers to see their gasoline. *©2000 Coolstock.com, Courtesy the General Petroleum Museum*

IOWA HIGHWAY MAP 1935

Phillips 66

Phillips 66

Compliments of
Phillips Petroleum Company

with a pair of visible pumps, this high-brow installation featured a dozen short, squat pumps, each encased in its own custom-built edifice. In concert, the pumping units evoked a feeling of opulence.

Instead of placing these gas pumping units at a central service island, the Atlantic Refining Company placed them along the two wings of an Ionic colonnade (the details of which were taken from the Erechtheum, the site where Athena waged war with Poseidon). To fill their tanks, motorists pulled into a circular driveway and parked in front of one of the pumps. Many cars could fit, accommodating multiple visitors at one time.

This eccentric pump installation may have been a harbinger of the changes to come. Within a few short years, the fast pace of improvements in the visible register's design contributed to its demise. Hand-cranks were no longer needed, as the introduction of electric motor pumps in 1923 eliminated the chore. With a speedier pump rate now possible, the time-consuming procedure of moving gas into a raised cylinder and releasing it into a fuel tank began to look like a waste of time. Increasingly, customers showed loyalty to a refiner's brand, rather than to how their gas looked. Speed and convenience were becoming more important than visual inspection. Everyone was in a hurry and wanted "fast gas."

In 1923, the motoring public got what they were asking for when L.O. and N.A. Carlson of Erie Meter Systems came out with high-speed electric-meter pumps. This was speedy pumping at its best, as the trend-setting dispensers used powerful electric motors capable of moving 15 gallons per minute at an accurate level of measurement. Because their round indicators resembled the familiar face of a clock dial, this elegant machine came to be known as the "clockface." The "hour" hand pointed to the gallon and the "minute" hand read out increments of a gallon.

Despite their utility, these electric-meter gas pumps were quickly outmoded. Robert Jauch, then chief engineer for the Wayne Pump Company, was busy working on a radical new "totalizer" (gallon vs. price calculator) in the early 1930s. He teamed up *continued on page 54*

DINO THE SINCLAIR DINOSAUR

Dino, the Sinclair dinosaur, was an idea hatched in 1930 during the height of the Great Depression. Advertising men working for the Sinclair Oil Company expressed an interest in capitalizing on the extremely "aged" Pennsylvania crudes that the company refined at their Wellsville, New York, facility. These pockets of oil were laid down more than 270 million years ago, during the Mesozoic era–a time when oversized reptiles ruled.

Eager to secure an admirable mascot, Sinclair's management staff went wild over the dinosaur idea and was quite agreeable to the stone-age association. The advertising department was given the green light to popularize a philosophy based on the claim that the "older the crude, the better the oils produced from it."

Sinclair's creative team proceeded with a carefully planned series of advertisements published in 100 newspapers and 5 magazines. Each featured a picture of a dinosaur–either Tyrannosaurus Rex, Triceratops, Stegosaurus, or Brontosaurus. The carnivorous tyrant Tyrannosaurus Rex was quite memorable. The Triceratops, with its trio of horns and tank-like appearance, commanded attention. With its spiked tail and armor plates, the Stegosaurus conjured up an image of strength. However, it was the Brontosaurus that people identified with the most. Like the Flintstone's family pet, it was viewed as docile (but strong), friendly, and loyal.

Out of the 12 creatures selected for the campaign, the docile vegetarian garnered the most amount of attention. Soon, Brontosaurus became the became public's favorite creature. Of course, Sinclair and the ad men were thrilled. Here was a mascot that had it all—the brontosaurus represented power, endurance, and stamina—while appealing to the majority of consumers. To Sinclair's delight, motorists nick-named the oversized animal "Dino," without any particular promotion. In no time at all, Dino the Brontosaurus held a position as the company's new mascot and advertising glamour boy.

The positive feelings created by the new mascot led the Sinclair refining company to their most successful promotion, the dinosaur stamp booklet. In 1935, motorists rushed to the nearest Sinclair station to collect a series of prehistoric stamp images. Each week, Sinclair stations issued a new stamp in a series of 12. Kids and adults marveled at the cool dinosaur images and eagerly pasted them into an educational picture album.

Almost immediately, the frenzy to collect the free dinosaur stamps and albums reached critical mass. After a single network radio broadcast detailing the offer was aired, the first printing was snapped up within 48 hours! When the popular dinosaur stamp promotion came to a close, over four million booklets in all had been distributed, decorated with some 48 million dinosaur stamps! Gasoline sales increased dramatically for Sinclair, and in 1932, Dino was officially registered as a company trademark.

One year later, P.G. Alen, a creator of life-like papier-mâché animals for motion pictures, began building a gigantic dinosaur diorama for the Century of Progress Exhibition in Chicago. The authenticity of this display led to the first company-sponsored geological materials for schools, libraries and home study. After distributing hundreds of thousands of copies, Sinclair Oil was utilizing its dinosaur theme for public education.

To empower these new materials with academic credentials, Sinclair financed the dinosaur fossil expeditions of Dr. Barnum Brown, then curator

"Dino the Dinosaur" was a popular mascot for the Sinclair Oil Company. This reproduction of a visible pump was once a main point of attraction for Walter Mears' Florida gas station. ©*2000 Marty Lineen, Jr.*

of fossil reptiles at the American Museum of Natural History. After Brown's death in 1963, Sinclair enlisted the help of Dr. John H. Ostrom of Yale University's Peabody Museum of Natural History. Ostrom continued Dr. Brown's research and acted as a consultant for the paleontology exhibit that was being built for the 1954 New York World's Fair.

A big fanfare accompanied the nine life-sized dinosaurs as they were slowly barged 125 miles down the Hudson river to the site of the New York World's Fair (one year before opening day). A huge banner painted with the words "Sinclair Dinosaurs on way to N.Y. World's Fair" piqued the public's interest. The major media picked up on the event,

too. Watching from the riverbanks, people knew that this exhibit was going to be special.

Of course, this scientifically accurate re-enactment of life during the Mesozoic age featured the ever-popular Dino. He proved to be one of the most popular exhibits at the fair, just as he had done so admirably along the roadsides of America. Between 1964 and 1965, nearly 10 million excited visitors jammed Sinclair's New York World's Fair pavilion to learn about the Earth's history and observe creatures from another time. Dino the Sinclair dinosaur was there, towering above it all, the star of the show.

Gilmore passed the overhead reduction on to the public. As the large, neon sign said: "Gilmore, Serve Yourself. Save Five Cents Per Gallon." People did just that, and Los Angeles led the nation in the creation of self-serve pumping.

But there was more to it than just a large number of gasoline pumps. Pump island layout was exceedingly important, something that *Architectural Record* addressed in 1944. In "The Gasoline Filling and Service Station," columnist K. Lonberg Holm raised a valid point when he wrote that "pump accessibility is the most important factor to be considered in the layout of the station." The point stressed for many architects was that the driveways "should give a direct approach to the pumps," from the street.

Two old pumps and one abandoned station. These days, it's rare to find any unused pumps in their "natural" environment. Collectors have ravaged the roadsides for all of the petroliana they could possibly find. ©2000 Coolstock.com

Outside of Fort Worth, Texas, this retired Phillips pump harkens back to a time when the standalone pump was king, the customer was always right, and gas was cheap. ©2000 Coolstock.com

At the time, it was recommended that station designers build pump islands so that one bank of pumps served two driveways. On one island there were three gasoline pumps or two tandem pumps. These pumps provided two filler hoses for ordinary gas and two for high-grade. Fuel pumping speed was generally accepted at 7 to 8 gallons per minute for hand-operated pumps and 15 to 20 gallons per minute for the motor-operated pumps. Dispensing gasoline had turned into a science!

For the height of the pump island, station builders adhered to a common standard. During the 1940s and 1950s, concrete pads on which pumps were mounted were not less than 6 inches high to prevent the possibility of cars colliding with the pumps. All edges of the pad were to be rounded and where space was limited, the pumping platforms had to follow the driveway curve.

Of course, everyone knew that that the pump island was literally the display and deal counter of the gas station. The service station attendant really shined

Two Wayne 60 gas pumps mark the spot of this closed gas station on Highway 54, outside of Wichita, Kansas. It's sad to see that the small-time stations, such as this one, will never be open again. Ya'll come back now, ya hear? ©2000 Coolstock.com

The gasoline pump as an architectural mirror. Throughout the years, the gasoline pumps of America followed the styling changes of architecture and design. ©2000 Coolstock.com

Ain't that America? Clapboard siding, an individual gas pump, and the ever-present air hose: all common elements of the classic service station of old. ©2000 Coolstock.com

between the pumps, packing racks full of motor oil, anti-freeze, and numerous other car accessories and displaying the goods where motorists could see them. Decades before convenience stores, the pump island generated the majority of the gas station revenue and was viewed with almost holy reverence.

For that reason, many of the leading gas pump manufacturers of the day introduced specialized gas pumps. These unique pumps were constructed so that their bodies were larger than the ordinary gas pump's and were wide enough to house a small display case. Behind a glass door, station owners could stock all sorts of goods and effectively market them to customers—without taking away precious space at the pump island. It was a great solution for the station that used a minimum amount of real estate.

During the mid-1930s, Tokheim debuted a line of display case pumps that were quite popular. With dramatic art deco styling, the Model 36B was a single-hose pump with space reserved for a "jumbo sales case" below the price calculator. This case could hold quite a bit: it was 13-1/2 inches wide, 24 inches high, and 4-1/8 inches deep. A hinged glass door protected goods from the elements and allowed the attendant to restock quickly.

Gas stations could take advantage of the display case option on both sides of the pump. The typical unit had a couple of shelves attached inside the box, allowing proprietors to showcase oil cans, tire patch kits, fan belts, spark plugs, and replacement lamps. To illuminate the point-of-purchase gas pump, Tokheim came out with the "Stationlighter," an 11-foot pump-top extension that held a reflector and light bulb above the dispenser. It was great for pulling in business at night, a time when business dropped off because of inadequate lighting.

Tokheim also developed the Model 36ADC: an impressive, extra-wide accessory pump with more than double the storage capacity of the single unit. This version boasted hinged glass doors on both the front and sides, with indirect lighting from above. With product visible from all four sides, managers went wild with this model. It was roomy enough to store batteries, large containers of anti-freeze, transmission oil, canisters of grease, and more.

The desire to sell automotive accessories at the pump spurred many other pump manufacturers to design and manufacture display case pumps of their

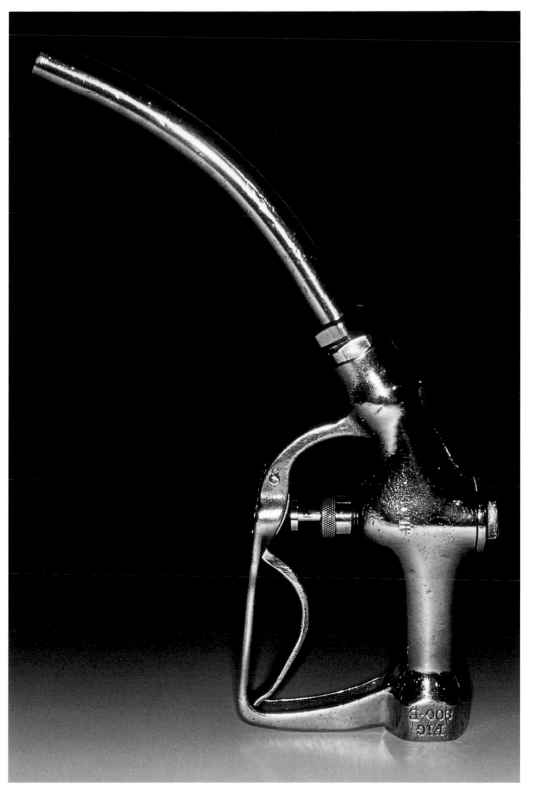

The pump handle made of solid brass was the standard issue at gas stations across the land. Decades ago, there were no rubber boots or emission-control gadgets to limit the evaporation of fumes as gas entered the tank. ©2000 Coolstock.com

A GAS PUMP THAT THINKS

In 1932, gas stations relied on visible register and clockface pumps to measure gasoline. Neither method could tell the pump operator or customer the final price. If an attendant saw that a customer pumped 10 gallons, he checked a price chart to get the final cost. It was slow, prone to error, and a waste of time.

All of that changed when engineer Bob Jauch, employed by the Wayne Pump Company in Fort Wayne, Indiana, began working on a gadget that not only measured the flow of gas, but read out the price as well. As the story goes, Jauch was pals with one of the sales reps at Veeder-Root, a company that had the technical and manufacturing capabilities to build such a device. He decided to drop in at the Hartford, Connecticut, facility to take a look.

After a few days of perusing the plant facilities, Jauch met with company officials and revealed that Wayne was planning to develop a new type of meter device for pumps. As he went on to explain, Veeder-Root was the likely candidate to manufacture it—taking into account their experience and reputation in the field. It just so happened that the Veeder-Root Company was working on a similar idea. Ed Slye, the Veeder-Root engineer, took a look at Jauch's prototype and came to the matter-of-fact conclusion that it was "nothing more than a gear box." After a careful analysis of Wayne's prototype, Slye announced that he could design a "variator" that was simpler, more economical, and better performing.

Jauch was stunned by the statement and quickly withdrew from the deal. He consulted with Wayne's president, Bill Griffin, who countered by saying that the Wayne Pump Company should get credit for any improvements Veeder-Root made on their original designs. Once legal matters were put into order, gearing wizard Slye began his work. Within a very short time, the company had what they called their new "eight-inch computer." Because of Jauch's preliminary work on the calculating device, the "Slye Patent" was assigned to the Wayne Pump Company.

At the time, Wayne was the only pump manufacturer to install the new device in their pumps. They were Veeder-Root's only customer for the new computer. Marketing met strong resistance when it solicited the other pump companies to switch over from the outmoded dial face designs to the more accurate mechanical calculator. The larger oil companies acted like they had no interest, cognizant of the fact that Veeder-Root's new measuring instrument rendered current pumping equipment obsolete.

Nobody else had a product that could compare with the new eight-inch computer, so they tried to freeze the calculator out of the market. It didn't really matter, since the Wayne Pump Company knew they were holding a royal flush. To play their hand and make it pay off handsomely, they concentrated on selling the improved pumps to independent service stations and oil companies.

As part of an aggressive marketing campaign, panel trucks with fully assembled gasoline pumps mounted in the rear toured the country. Not surprisingly, the independents liked what they saw and orders began to pour in. With their eyes wide open in amazement, lessees under the thumb of the major oil refiners questioned why they had to use inaccurate, outdated machinery. They began to complain and companies were forced to upgrade.

In order to avoid paying royalties to Wayne, a few of the other big gas pump makers tried their best to duplicate the invention. Unfortunately for them, all of the calculators turned out to be spin-offs from the original patent, copying its central design. After a few lawsuits and failed attempts, all of the remaining 12 pump manufacturers fell into line and licensed the new computer variator. The days of the visible register and clockface were over.

With a "Head for Figures," Wayne's new line of computer calculator gasoline pumps proved to be a major improvement in the functionality of fuel delivery. Wherever operators installed it, the mechanical calculator changed the way fuel was sold. Instead of reading a dial-face indicator on a clockface unit and having to figure out the cash total, a station attendant simply glanced at the number wheels and announced the price.

Automatically, a beehive of tiny gears and wheels spun around inside the gas pump variator, totaling the gallons and then displaying the numbers in dollar amount. As a welcome by-product of this new pumping arrangement, customer confidence bloomed. The chance for operator error and dishonesty had been reduced.

Gasoline was no longer sold in amounts of $1 or $2. Average sales increased dramatically, especially when 39 cents became 38-8/10 cents—it sounded cheaper! For the first time in gas pump history, "Shall I fill 'er-up?" became the standard question at America's gas stations. Customers loved it, and the gasoline flowed like never before.

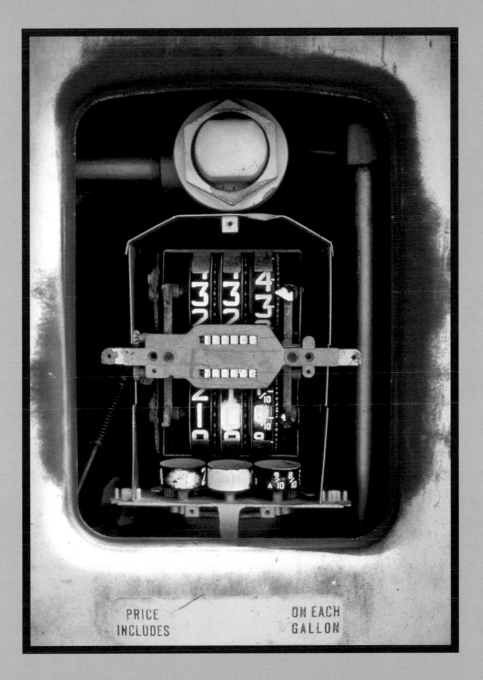

Exposed, the inner workings of this retired pump disclose the secrets behind the calculation of price. Gears, wheels, and other mechanisms comprised the magic. ©2000 Coolstock.com

own. Within a few years, most of the major pump makers had merchandising models. The gas pump island had become a sales office.

In 1939, gas pump engineers grabbed the spotlight from the merchandising men when they began to address some of the problems with the pump section. For years, moisture and sediment constantly plagued the gasoline held in underground storage tanks. This was before the days of efficient filters, and even the best straining devices couldn't keep the gasoline and pumps free from fine silt or moisture. When the liquid passed through the typical meter, the swirling action caused a vortex, which forced the impurities to the bottom. This caused the crankshaft ball-bearing raceway to bind and the pump would fail. Many times, the pump cylinders would bind as well, leading to failure.

Fortunately, the Bennett Pump Company found a solution to this problem when they joined forces with the engineering staff of Sinclair Refining Company.

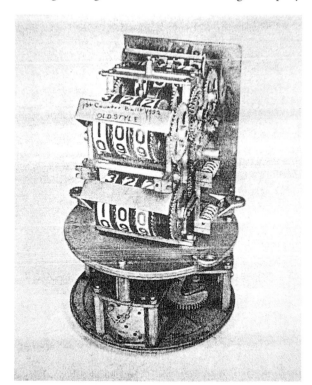

After the clever gasoline pump calculator was perfected, gas pump operators could easily figure out the price. Customers could now say "give me five dollars' worth" instead of "give me ten gallons of gas." It was a major achievement. *Courtesy Tokheim Corporation*

A close-up view of the gas pump handle; a device that has seen countless motorists lift it from the pump, flip up the lever, and squeeze a few gallons into the tank.
©2000 Coolstock.com

Working together, they produced one of the finest pump and meter dispensing systems known to the industry. They called the combo of base, pump, eliminator, and meter assembly the "Pyramid Construction." In 1940, they debuted this new "540 Series" at the company's general sales meeting.

For the next few years, gas pump state-of-the-art advanced only marginally. The mechanical aspect of the pumping mechanism remained almost the same while design improvements were made to the calculating head. When submerged pumps came on the scene, the height of the pump cabinets decreased. During the late 1950s, a mechanical incremental blender was developed by Einer Young, an engineer with Sun Oil Company. It allowed gas stations to market "custom blended" gas right at the pumps. Some motorists viewed the one-pump blender suspiciously, since they couldn't be sure of the mix or what was flowing from the hose.

When the gas grade selector dial pump debuted, many motorists were skeptical of what came out of the pump hose. Who could be sure that it wasn't all the same grade of gas? ©2000 Coolstock.com

This crumbling Wayne 60 gas pump is a prime example of the Art Deco influences seen in the gas pumps of an earlier age. Pumps were often miniaturized recreations of grand architectural constructions. ©2000 Coolstock.com

63

PA 115—The Turnpike's Picturesque Midway Inn and Service Station at Bedford
"America's Dream Highway"

At the Midway Inn, the gas pumps were easily spotted by motorists at night. Elevated lamp posts at each pumping station lit the way for customers at all hours. *Courtesy Coolstock.com*

STOPPING OFF FO[R]
A LITTLE RELAXATION
ALONG THE WAY!

Pulling up to the pumps gave motorists of yesteryear a chance to stretch their legs and relax. Taking a quick puff on a cigar—while in the rest room—was a big pastime, especially if the wife disapproved of the habit. *Courtesy Coolstock.com*

70

comply with the edict and discontinue the sale of gasoline with these classic pumpers. Before it was all said and done, the only visible-register pumps that remained were those used for agricultural purposes.

A new Environmental Protection Agency edict called for the updating of all underground storage tanks. Supposedly, leaky gasoline storage tanks were polluting public water supplies. Suddenly, stations that took in a modest amount in sales were required to invest hundreds of thousands of dollars in new tanks. As is evidenced by today's small number of independent gas stations, many did not.

As the decade of disco fell to the 1980s, individual pump cabinets saw their demise. Gasoline

The classic house-style station still exists in Chandler, Oklahoma. The three-pump format was a common configuration at many gas stations across the nation. ©2000 Coolstock.com

WHY THEY CALLED IT 66

Among the myriad gasoline trademarks that once colored America's main streets, no brand of motor fuel has been saddled with as much controversy as Phillips 66 gasoline. Since their first gallon of gasoline gurgled up to fill a visible register pump, there has been endless puzzlement over their choice of name. Why, people wondered, was their gasoline brand designated with "66?"

The most common explanation is based on numerical myth. This overworked fable recalls the details surrounding the opening of the first Phillips station in Wichita, Kansas. According to the legend, the flagship refueling station was reputed to have sold 6,600 gallons of gas by the end of the first day's business. As the story goes, the station manager turned to a company rep (who just happened to be standing nearby) and said, "Boy, 66 is our lucky number!" Unfortunately, the truth is that the first Phillips station pumped more than 12,000 gallons of motor fuel during its grand opening.

One bizarre tale boasts of high-stakes gamblers and luck: According to legend, a Phillips official won the company's first Texas panhandle petroleum refinery in a game of dice. The owner of the facility rolled "double sixes" in an unlucky toss and lost it all. Back in Bartlesville, company directors liked those unlucky boxcars so much that they named the refinery's product "Phillips 66." A colorful episode, but also false. Most likely, this originates from the oil distillery's neighbor, the 6666 Ranch, which was reportedly won in a poker game with a hand of four sixes.

Another fictional fallacy that tries to explain the origin of the Phillips 66 brand is that Frank and L.E. Phillips, prior to founding the company, had only $66 left when their first successful oil well struck black gold.

Because of the timing of their strike, they decided that if they ever marketed gasoline to motorists, it would be called "Phillips 66."

Sounds pretty believable, but it's not true. While it is generally known that the Phillips brothers stressed their finances to the limit with their oil explorations, there is no evidence that the company name shows the dollar amount of capital remaining when their Anna Anderson oil well blackened the sky as an Oklahoma gusher.

A few scientifically oriented scenarios have been perpetuated to explain the name, including the unfounded report that Phillips 66 gasoline had an octane rating of 66; or that its much-touted "controlled volatility" was perfected after 66 lab tests. The truth is, no one knows for sure how many experiments were performed, not even the company. Plus, the methods for determining octane weren't adopted until five years after the trademark selection.

The true story of Phillips 66 gasoline began in 1927, when the first gallon was offered for sale in Wichita, Kansas. For months, preparations for the grand opening had kept employees busy. In business for only 10 years, Phillips was previously involved only in the production of crude oil. Now, it was venturing into the consumer market for the very first time. In the rush to make their formula perfect, little thought was given to selecting an appropriate name. Down to the wire, they were stumped.

Company officials knew one thing: the name for Phillips' new motor fuel had to sound "catchy." Somehow, the name had to have a hook that would cause consumers to remember it. As marketing was well aware, a brand identifier with pizzazz stood a better chance of capturing the motorist's attention at the pumps.

The Phillips 66 brand name is shrouded with fable and mystery. Many myths have been perpetuated to explain its origin for inquiring motorists. ©2000 Coolstock.com

In an effort to meet these guidelines, Phillips researchers recommended using the benchmark for implying quality in that era, something referred to as "high gravity." Because the gravity of the new gasoline was very close to the number 66, chemists working in the research department suggested that these numerals be used for the moniker. It sounded like the perfect choice.

Nevertheless, scientists analyzed the logic too long. After some debate, they came to the conclusion that a name linked to one specific gravity wouldn't go well with Phillips' marketing plan. One number didn't work well with the concept of "varying gravity and controlling volatility to fit a range of seasons." Once this final idea was discarded, a special committee was organized for the sole purpose of determining the new trademark. On the

night of the planned meeting, a Phillips company official was on his way back to the Bartlesville headquarters in a company car—an automobile that was being used to road test their new motor fuel. That's where fate stepped in: "This car goes like 60 on our new gas!" announced the official. "60 nothing," answered the driver, "We're doing 66!"

Later—at the meeting—somebody asked where this dialogue occurred. Wouldn't you know it: "Near Tulsa, on Highway 66." No doubt, a collective shiver ran up and down the backs of all in attendance. With haste, the executives took a vote and reached a unanimous decision: Phillips Petroleum would kick off the sale of its powerful new gasoline under the distinctive brand "Phillips 66." The Mother Road—and the speed of a test car—made it so.

The gas station attendant dressed in white attire was a potent representation of the company brand. Cleanliness and neatness in regard to appearance went a long way toward strengthening the bond between customer and brand. *Courtesy Shell Oil Company*

Ellensburg, Washington, was the home of Floyd Wipple's gas station. Twenty years ago, this was the place motorists visited when they wanted the full service treatment. Sadly, Floyd has passed on, and his friendly gas station is just another fond entry in the annals of the American gas station. *©2000 Coolstock.com*

The station attendant's shoes were moved to a new level as well. The axiom of "you can tell what kind of a man he is by the shoes he wears" was put to the test with leather boots, trimmed out with a pair of matching leather shin guards. From all appearances, the gas station attendant was ready to go into battle. Here was the roadside gladiator of a new age, one who championed the needs of the car owner while upholding the prize of dependability.

But there was more to being an effective gas station employee than just throwing on a fancy uniform. The best personalities suited for the job were the gregarious types that liked to talk and wanted to listen. Part family doctor and part psychologist, the station man had to be ready to hear all sorts of stories about cars and remain interested as customer upon customer shared their problems. Attending to the public and their cars wasn't a job for someone who didn't like people.

To become a respected gas station attendant meant dedication to the service of others and having a conscientious spirit. You had to be a friendly sort of

REGULAR

UNLEADED

REGULAR

character with the public relation skills of an ambassador! In 1937, this personality was indicated by the smiling visage of a service station attendant imprinted on the October cover of *The Shield*, a Phillips 66 magazine. If one viewed the cover at "face value," a warm grin showing a prodigious amount of teeth was worthy enough to be recognized as "The Phillips Smile."

During the height of America's motoring years, the gasoline station attendant had a lot to smile about, for he was more than just a pump operator. In addition to his refueling duties, he acted as a part-time mechanic and salesman. From his position at the driver's side window, he took every available opportunity to extol the virtues of various types of motor oil, anti-freeze, bug spray, transmission fluid, and batteries. His duties were all-encompassing and his knowledge of motorcars was impressive.

Customer safety was a primary concern: after checking your tires for the correct air pressure, the smiling service man suggested that you buy a new set of treads or perform a tire rotation, if needed. If the

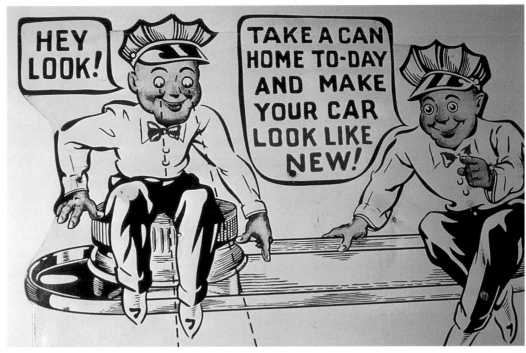

The image of a service attendant was often used to sell automotive products such as wax and detergent. ©2000 Coolstock.com

Gulf stations of the early 1910s relied on a rag-tag team of station workers to get the job done. Station portraits as this are commonplace, depicting the unharmonious image that many stations portrayed in their infancy. *Photograph provided, and reprinted with permission, by Chevron Corporation and its subsidiary, Chevron U.S.A. Inc.*

UNDER THE WINGS
OF THE FLYING **A**

Protection a mother appreciates

A mother's first thought is protection for her family...
that's why she stops at the "Flying A" for service
and "Flying A" Ethyl gasoline. Its instant response...its smooth
quiet power inspires confidence as she deftly drives through traffic.

Extra protection—extra power too, with Veedol 10-30—
the all season Motor Oil that gives highest octane performance.
Drive in at the sign of the "Flying A"...for power...
for safety service—and charge it all on your "Flying A" Credit Card.

FLYING **A** ETHYL

VEEDOL 10-30 MOTOR OIL cuts carbon deposits
—curbs pre-ignition...adds up to 40 extra miles to
every tankful of gasoline.

Painted by John McClelland for Tidewater Oil Company

TIDEWATER OIL COMPANY · San Francisco · Houston · Tulsa · New York

Under the wings of the Flying A, mothers found protection that they could appreciate. Flying A service and Ethyl gasoline gave women the confidence to drive deftly and smoothly through traffic. *Coolstock.com Collection*

jam glasses? The pump man at your neighborhood Gulf station had boxes of it in the back room. As your tank filled with fuel, he was ready, willing, and able to trade for the greenbacks handed through the driver's window. A great gift to pick up at the neighborhood Socony station were Tavern Lustre Cloths, along with insect killers such as Bug-a-Boo moth crystals and Bug-a-Boo insect spray (an early repellent that was rich in DDT). As the attendant hawked handy home oilers, his many customers recognized (without malice) him as an unabashed merchandiser, a goodwill emissary who was unashamed when it came to presenting new products and services.

The familiar and striking Texaco disc was part of the station re-imaging campaign designed by Walter Dorwin Teague. Mounted atop a slender pole, this bold star announced to motorists that Texaco gasoline was for sale beneath it. ©2000 Coolstock.com

One of the most useful items passed out by service station attendants across the nation were road maps. The craze began in 1914 when advertising executive William Adkin convinced the Gulf Oil company that they should distribute free maps to their customers. Ten thousand residents of Pennsylvania's Allegheny County received the first round of maps. Gulf's first drive-in station received a boost in business with the mailout and they quickly decided to expand the program. Soon, there were Gulf maps of surrounding New England states—a total of 300,000 distributed by year's end!

As the service station map idea flourished, a number of map-making companies sprang up. The Rand McNally Company printed its first road map in 1904 and the General Drafting Company made its debut in 1912 with a state map of Vermont. In the mid-1920s, a group of Rand McNally employees

At one time, Mobil offered Tavern Novelty candles as an extra item during the Christmas season. This station took the interior display to the maximum level, making it clear the products were a big part of its overall sales plan.
Courtesy A. J. Vogel

Oil cans were dispensed by the gas jockeys of days gone by. Motorists selected the brand they wanted, and the attendant poured it into the crankcase as part of the service. ©2000 Coolstock.com

WICKENBURG GASOLINE

If you ever find yourself traveling by car through Arizona along the old Phoenix Highway, or Route 60 as they call it, be sure to keep an eye peeled for the defunct Brumm's gas station located just outside of Wickenburg. It's a little difficult to spot because the roadbed was improved back in 1937 and relegated the former gas station to near obscurity.

In the span of a few years, the roadbed was elevated almost 50 feet, cutting off all visual contact with passing traffic. By that time, even the yellow and blue gull that adorned the Seaside brand gasoline signs couldn't pull in enough customers and sales dropped. By 1940, the gas pumps were shut down and two of the 250 gallon storage tanks were dug up. The situation looked grim and former customers mourned the loss of their local refueler.

Fortunately, the Brumm clan decided not to hang up their hoses and gas pump nozzles quite that easily. Instead of bowing to defeat by closing their filling station doors and moving on, they merged gracefully into an entirely new line of work! The old road out front was thick with tourists; a feeder highway to the old Mother Road, Route 66. It was a car conduit that could be readily tapped for other types of revenue.

As it turned out, selling curios and Indian jewelry became a more lucrative trade than the gasoline game. The former gasoline stop found a new purpose as a curio shop and managed to carve out a life for itself along the highway. By the 1980s, Hank Brumm was in command of the old gas station turned antique store—spending his days weaving his imaginative lore of the open road and selling Indian Squash-blossom jewelry to the tourists.

Inside the large antique shop, the Brumm family takes care to display a myriad of interesting knick-knacks, each with its own particular story. As a matter of fact, Hank makes it a point to highlight certain items that he likes to talk about, especially those that poke fun at some of our human foibles. A small trio of carpet tacks glued upright under a small, wooden house frame is one of his favorite novelties. With a wry smile covering his face, he can't resist revealing this personal "tax-shelter" to anyone who strays near it. He gets a kick out of it every time.

Some say that Hank has the business of the roadside in his blood. It's probably true, as he can still remember his younger days as a boy working on the old visible register pumps, toiling under the hot Arizona sun, servicing Studebaker straight eights, Ford Model As, and curved-dash Oldsmobiles with gasoline and motor oil.

For the locals, the station was the hub of excitement during the 1930s, especially when Wickenburg's main power plant failed. Equipped with the older-style, hand-cranked pumps, the Brumm's station rose to the occasion and was immune to the lack of electrical juice that shut down the newer, motorized pumps.

Today, antique collectors and petroliana enthusiasts are drawn in by the magic of the pumps. Not a day goes by without someone offering Hank or his mother, Elsie, all kinds of money to cart the pumps away

The scene at the Wickenburg, Arizona, gas station is one worthy of a time warp. Vintage visible register pumps recall the heyday of service. ©2000 Coolstock.com

and restore them in the name of "preservation." But brother Omar Brumm likes them just the way they are and wouldn't feel right to sell them. To him, the pumps are his old friends. Caked with a weather-worn patina of time and memories, they make him feel good when he glances out of the window.

Unfazed by the hubbub, Elsie still putters around the shop and makes a few sales when she can. As a young woman, she worked at a mercantile shop in Wickenburg. There, she discovered her skill for selling. One time, a wooden jewelry box arrived containing an old upper dental plate.

She decided to make a funny sign and display it in the window. Suddenly, a man rushed in and inquired whether the choppers were for sale. Elsie agreed on a price and he popped them in his mouth! Later, she realized that if she put her mind to it, she could sell almost anything.

And that's how the Brumm's gas station began. Elsie turned her talents to the road, altered her plans when it was necessary, and persevered. She passed on her legacy of endurance to her sons. For the people of Wickenburg, she set a vivid example of how the American dream can force a living; a life from the road.

The gas station attendants that appeared on the maps were equally handsome. Regardless of the brand, the attendant was shown as a helpful friend who answered any and all questions with patience. More often than not, he was seen pointing the way to nearby roadside attractions. His chiseled features set him apart as a rugged breed; a fraternity member who wasn't afraid of hard work and helping others. Of course, there were no grizzled beards, pot bellies, or bald heads to be seen here! The service station attendant was a real man's man—the kind who shaved with a straight razor and splashed on a lot of English Leather.

While many stations showed an occasional farm animal or pet on their map covers, the early examples of these road guides were strangely devoid of children.

Pictured here is a Phil Pete statue, a Phillips coin bank, and an attendant service award; all celebrating the station man and petrol worker stereotype. ©2000 Coolstock.com

spun off their own cartographic enterprise and called it the J. M. Gousha Company. All three of these companies played a prominent role in the creation of maps for America's service stations. In the process, they captured the art and style of a bygone era and encapsulated the best of motoring and refueling cars on the printed page.

Of all the items given out by the service station attendant, the road map was the most important. Today, gas station maps provide researchers with important data about the development and maturation of our roads, as well as fads and fashions of the day.

Many of the earliest maps glamorized the motoring hobby to the extreme. Usually, couples were seen in large, powerful rag tops, asking for directions or waiting as their gasoline tank was refilled. Oil refiners were proud of their image and the service station portrait was a common theme. Of course, beautiful people were always depicted on map covers, most notably well-dressed women. Here again, the car was typically a convertible and you could feel the wind in the driver's hair. With happy smiles on their faces and tussled locks, fresh-faced beauties zoomed into the hinterlands to explore. By this time, the automobile, and purchasing gas, was so foolproof that there was no need for a man!

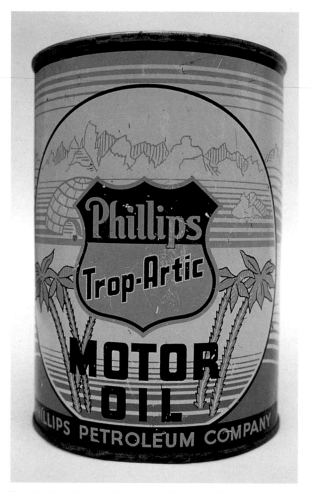

The Phillips Trop-Artic motor oil can—with palm trees—commands a high price in the current petroliana collector's market. A few years ago, cans were the standard in oil distribution. Now, plastic bottles with twist-off tops have taken over. ©2000 Coolstock.com

In 1954, Phillips organized its Employee Sales Assistance Program, which developed the cartoon characters Phil Pete and his girlfriend Phyllis to influence employees to use and sell Phillips products. The program broke new ground as a corporate moral booster, and had a major impact on the popularization of the gas company credit card. For every 10 active card accounts that an employee secured, they received a gold-colored statue of Phil Pete. ©2000 Coolstock.com

Whether it's driveway signs, gas pump globes, or oil drums, the Mobiloil name was a recognizable symbol along America's gasoline highways. Shown here is part of the collection at the Red Horse Museum in Augusta, Kansas. ©2000 Coolstock.com

ROADSIDE REST ROOMS

"If there's any place about a station that can lose customers in a hurry, it's an untidy rest room. It makes motorists boiling mad." So decreed the writer in a 1935 manual from Standard Oil of California. For decades, the roadside privy was the butt of jokes, a theme for humorous postcards, and the bane of the long-distance traveler. Visiting a toilet while "on the road" was no more civilized than it was during the days when motoring began.

Texaco was the first to combat the status quo in 1938 with their registered restrooms. Each unit was registered by the company and individually numbered. Behind doors labeled with green and white "men" and "ladies" placards, car customers found tiled interiors, modern commodes, and gleaming sinks with fresh soap and real towels. Cleanliness was actually "guaranteed!"

Touting these new facilities as "A Texaco Dealer Service," green and white curb signs were positioned out near the roadway where motorists wouldn't miss them. Texaco dealers even took an eight-point pledge to keep their restrooms clean. If they cared to, customers could read the creed while they were taking care of business for it was posted on the restroom wall.

To ensure that the new washrooms lived up to the hype, Texaco operated a fleet of 48 Chevrolet two-door coupes. Known as the "White Patrol," company inspectors roamed the 48 states to perform the white glove test—verifying that the gas station restroom was an amenity the automobile owner could rely on.

Texaco management found out that the super-clean concept had a great potential for attracting customers. In the 1947 issue of *Texaco Dealer*, the company writers bragged that "Probably no better tool for extracting money from tourists was ever devised than the Registered Rest Room." They were right on the money. People liked the idea of a public restroom that was sanitary.

Therefore, in 1939, the Phillips Petroleum company rolled out their version of the clean service station restroom. It kicked off the campaign by publishing the pamphlet, "A Challenge Beyond Evasion." They held true to the tone of the missive; moving into action by individually numbering all of the gas stations in their sales territory. Every station was to be officially "certified."

The company backed up the idea of cleanliness with muscle. To show Phillips meant business, they hired a team of registered nurses; a dedicated group of women drove around the countryside and personally examined the cleanliness of (and give the seal of approval) to bathrooms. Standards were set, and the uniformed team performed spot checks to ensure conformity.

Known as the "Highway Hostesses," they played double-duty as ambassadors for the company and helping promote Phillips 66 with their "courteous manner, pleasant personalities, and willingness to aid people in distress." With the utmost congeniality, the Highway Hostesses directed tourists to all of the "better" hotels, coffee shops, and other attractions. In their spare time, they discussed infant hygiene with traveling mothers. All of the Hostesses duties were performed under the watchful gaze of Matilda Passmore. A registered nurse and a "nationally-known health lecturer," Matilda was a tough cookie when it came to clean toilets.

As word of the Texaco Registered Restrooms and the Phillips Certified units spread, other oil companies joined the clean-up campaign. Gulf

The men's and women's restrooms were, and still are, an Important part of the roadside scene. While they may be more modern today, they were a lot more pristine when cleanliness programs to insure sanitation were in place. ©2000 Coolstock.com

promoted their "clean rest rooms" on service station roadmaps. Esso stations touted their facilities with something called the "Comfort Award;" a framed certificate that bragged, "OUR rest room is YOUR rest room while you are in it." A photo of a pristine commode and sink adorned the center of the award, along with the name and signature of the dealer.

Shell was a bit more imaginative and began its own campaign with ads in periodicals such as *Good Housekeeping*. Marjorie Illing, then Chairman of the General Federation of Women's Clubs, praised America's Shell gasoline dealers "on their prompt response to the pleas of *Good Housekeeping* magazine for sanitary equipment and better housekeeping in gasoline-station rest rooms." Labeled with a "White Cross of Cleanliness," Shell service station

managers assured motorists that their facilities were "Home-Clean!"

Sadly, the restroom cleanliness programs saw a slow demise during the late 1950s. At the time, Union Oil was promoting the "Sparkle Corps," a group of sexy stewardess lookalikes who spent the summer primping for photo opportunities and publicity events. No nurses were to be found in this crew; models, secretaries, and college girls were recruited for the summer to inspect plumbing.

In the end, all of the restroom programs faded from the scene and the public gasoline station toilets reverted to their former unkempt status. In the end, it was the station manager, owner, or kid working the register who was responsible for keeping the facilities clean. Restrooms no longer came with a guarantee.

Whatever you needed at the gas station, whether it was a tank of gas or a spare hubcap, the gas station attendant was there to provide and install it for you. ©2000 Coolstock.com

Out in the desert, Dad Lee's was once a landmark for motorists cruising into California. This attendant was a character; evidenced by the unique assembly of signs. *Courtesy Coolstock.com*

By the mid-1940s, some of the housewives who were collecting the stamps began handing them out, too! As the majority of men went off to battle in World War II, women moved in to ease the shortage of pump jockeys. As in every other industry, women added their own flair to the job and did the nation proud.

The female pump attendant followed fashion guidelines similar to her male counterpart, although the style varied according to region. In one area of the country, Standard Oil dressed up its women workers in attractive jumpsuits especially tailored for the female form. A red and white striped short-sleeve shirt was worn beneath, with an open collar. The cap was of the one piece military wedge variety, decorated with a single stripe.

In the SOHIO (Standard Oil of Ohio) region, female attendants donned dark blue dresses that featured contrasting piping on the pockets and collar.

At Elkhart Lake, Wisconsin, this classic Cities Service station had all that one could offer the motorist, including multiple garage bays for repairs and gas pumps for refueling. A great location for car service. *Courtesy Coolstock.com*

At Duncan's Shell Service and Restaurant, customers could fill their cars with gas and stoke up on some tasty grub. It's likely that the attendant here doubled as the short-order cook. *Courtesy Coolstock.com*

Known in the industry as Sohioettes, these women operators were among the most well-dressed in the industry. Only the registered nurses of the Phillips 66 Highway Hostesses and the women of Texaco's White Patrol equaled their appearance.

Man or woman, gas station attendants vied for praise on a job well done. Since the early inception of the gas station, oil refiners established a variety of incentive and reward programs. Depending on the total quantity of station sales, gallons sold, and customer input, the shining stars of the pumping world were many. Phillips 66 even had statuettes as awards for its best workers. These golden awards were highly coveted by the career gas station worker and station owner. In short order, they became the high octane equivalent to the Oscar.

To attain this level of excellence, teaching the art and style of the service station attendant was an ongoing concern. During the roaring 1920s, prospective pump jockeys began at their neighborhood station and learned the ropes from mentors. Books such as Charles Jones' *Service Station Management: Its Principles and Practices* were quite instructive for hopefuls. By the 1950s, the idea of working at a gas station was

so popular that high schools offered vocational courses. In New York City, classes such as "Fuel Oil Distribution" and "Service Station Management" were popular with students.

It was easy to see why these classes were so popular, as the service station of yesteryear was a place of varied activity. It was never boring at the gas station.

At the Milbank Auto Garage in South Dakota, specialized mechanics took care of repairing automobiles. Today, chain stores have usurped this role, offering specialized services ranging from tire repair to engine exchange. *Courtesy Coolstock.com*

One can just imagine the gas station attendant waiting inside this Standard Service station, eager to jump up from his chair, run out, pump some gas, and rent out a cabin. *Courtesy Coolstock.com*

While the primary activity was pumping gas, station attendants were entrusted with a variety of additional car duties. During the heyday of the service station, it wasn't unusual to see three or more attendants swoop down on a car for service. While one attendant wiped the windshield and cleared it of bugs and dirt, another paid attention to the tires. A third enshrined the question "Shall I check under the hood?" into the annals of history and worked on the engine. At this point, the oil dipstick was checked for proper level and the radiator for anti-freeze.

If the oil level was low or the radiator was low on coolant, the attendant reached for a branded can from the service station sales island and offered to replenish your tanks. Sure, you could go to the hardware store, buy the car care products, and do it yourself, but this guy knew what he was doing. He knew about oil and created an aura that convinced you he knew best for your car. In those days, there was little doubt to his honesty and customers often took the attendant's "suggestions" to heart.

These were the times when air was free and refill hoses were attached to compressors in the service bay. Who among us that has ever driven an automobile or rode a bicycle can forget the Ecco tire inflator device? Mounted to a wall near the garage door or perched atop a slender post, a control head regulated the pressure going into our tires. It was easy to use—all one had to do was turn the small chrome crank and set the numbers to the desired pressure. No need of a separate tire gauge here and no need to push coins into a money-grubbing machine.

But the days of the pay-as-you-go air machine were soon to come. After World War II, servicemen returned from overseas and took over the gas stations. The 1950s spurred an all-out boom in driving, and motorists took to the roads in masses to see the sights and to travel. As America entered the 1960s, changing attitudes toward authority slowly shifted. In the process, the work ethic changed and along with it, the qualities that were once important in the gas station

Along old Route 66, service facilities such as this Mother Road survivor were once commonplace. ©2000 Coolstock.com

Cans of Phillips motor oil were positioned in racks at the pump island where the motorists could see them, and request the Phillips brand of oil from the attendant on duty. ©*2000 Coolstock.com*

By the end of the 1970s, signs like these were getting more and more difficult to find. Gas stations all across America were ditching their service bays, and repairs had to be made at specialized service businesses. ©*2000 Coolstock.com*

This is where it all happened—the service bay of the typical American gas station garage. When they weren't pumping gas, attendants fixed flats, repaired motors, and did everything it took to get cars back on the road. *Courtesy A. J. Vogel*

THE DEATH OF SERVICE

Remember when filling stations fixed flat tires for just a few bucks? Before the advent of self-service pumps, gas stations had garage bays. Around the clock, attendants welcomed any and all repairs. Between pumping gas, wiping windows, and checking the oil, mechanics performed the duties that kept motorists going.

Today, this nostalgic picture worthy of a Norman Rockwell painting has evaporated like spilled fuel. The reason? Most of the roadside refueling stations that used to feature auto repair facilities have gone out of business. Like it or not, the mom-and-pop fix-it shop is no more. The discount tire house, department store repair garage, and franchised auto parts warehouse have assumed the noble task of fixing up our flivver.

As a rather unfortunate consequence, the time and effort it takes to get a mechanical problem repaired has increased. To get a car back in shape and on the road, consumers must confront a service backlog as long as a week! These days, automotive walk-in repairs are unheard of, and advance appointments are the norm.

Worse yet, the average repair bill is outlandish. Believe it or not, the hourly rate some car shops charge for mechanic's work rivals that of a degreed engineer! Ironically, Gus the gas station mechanic gets the short end of the dipstick—most of the profits are deposited into the garage owner's deep pockets.

To keep the modern-day customers happy while their cars are being serviced and credit cards are processed, waiting rooms are now standard. Equipped with color TVs, piles of magazines, and dispensers that sell overpriced snack food, they resemble the holding pen in a doctor's office. On any day of the week (and more so on weekends), waiting rooms can be found packed to the seams with customers—all waiting for their baby to come out of surgery.

Conditions are no better at most of the smaller gas stations. These days, it appears that most of the survivors along gasoline alley have become quite choosy when it comes to repair work. Many are reluctant to take on tasks deemed "unglamorous." Towing dead cars for the AAA has become a hot business prospect for many and much more profitable than engine repairs.

When that rare station is agreeable to fixing a flat, the cost is often considerable. The latest twist in pricing the repair of tires is what's referred to as the "added surcharge." What it means is that many of our nation's service stations are tacking on an extra charge to penalize motorists for using one of the most helpful motoring accessories devised by man: Fix-a-Flat.

For those car owners unschooled in spur-of-the-moment repair, Fix-a-Flat is a pressurized sealant-in-a-can that has saved many a commuter from trouble and delivered them safely to the nearest garage for a permanent repair. A convenient way to plug up a leak while in transit, Fix-a-Flat has risen from relative obscurity to become a boon to the car owner and bane to the service station.

Much to the chagrin of motorists who find it useful, station owners, mechanics, and attendants recoil at the mere mention of it! If the substance is found to be "gunking up" the interior of your tire, most tire repair shops will think nothing of charging you an extra fee to make the repair.

The reason? According to a major service station recently patronized by this writer, Fix-a-Flat is "flammable and hazardous." A curious

Clare Patterson ran a gas station in Augusta, Kansas, for a good number of years. Later, he opened the Red Horse Museum. These days, he's content to watch the traffic go by and reminisce about the early days of service. Patterson is the last of his kind, dedicated to the ethics of a forgotten art. ©2000 Coolstock.com

statement since the container states just the opposite. According to the hyperbole spouted by many a station repair person, "a horrendous explosion could result when the tire is taken off the rim." Because of this, hazardous duty pay is warranted when a flat-fixer encounters a sealed-up tire.

Of course, the ardent fans of Fix-a-Flat know that this line of thinking is pure poppycock. The real reason that America's station repair workers don't like the stuff is that it works far *too* well. With a Fix-a-Flat treated tire, a heck of a lot more time will be spent looking for a puncture hole—precious time that could be better spent engaging in far more lucrative activities.

If we are to believe the mechanic, we should all forget about using that can of Fix-a-Flat we all have stashed away in our trunks. When stranded by a flat tire, it's our duty as a car owner to change the tire and risk all of the dangers of being hit by another car. Isn't that part of the excitement of motoring?

So the next time you find yourself riding on the rim, try to hold off on using the Fix-a-Flat. Take the time to dig out that dirty spare and rusty old jack. Turn adversity into opportunity and relearn the wonders of dismounting a tire! Get down on your knees and loosen lug bolts. Not only will your neighborhood gas station attendant thank you, but so will your wallet.

The venerable gas station attendant, caught in a candid moment, doing the job that he does best–filling an automobile's tank with gasoline. ©2000 Coolstock.com

enlighten the audience with his opinions about the extinction of America's small businesses—including dialog on patriotism, the ecology, gender issues, and global ethics. To keep it interesting, he selects subjects from the "hub cap story wheel" and at a moment's notice, changes the course of his entertaining monologue. Unfortunately, the likable character known as "Sonny" is only a stage persona perpetuated by Benny Reehl, former gas station attendant.

Founder of Creative Reehlizations, a Maine-based production company specializing in the various

venues popular theater has used throughout the twentieth century, Reehl has been involved with a variety of theatrical forms. Much of his onstage acting experience was gained as a "parlor entertainer," performing solo in hotels, saloons, town halls, and parlors of private homes for small-town residents. The "Chautauqua" became his favorite form and provided the early framework for his current production.

However, the actual concept of the "Service Station Museum" was taken directly from Sonny's life. Reehl grew up around the service station and the atmosphere that made it so special. He pumped his first gallon of gas when he was only 14 years old and thoroughly enjoyed the customers and conversations. He was so at home in the automotive work environment that he chose to work at service stations until well into his 20s.

Years ago, when he first discovered that manufacturers were producing parts that couldn't be repaired (such as sealed batteries and radiators and non-greasable parts), he realized that the gas station business was doomed for extinction. When self-service gasoline became the status quo, he began to notice that customers raced in and out of his station with little time for small talk. Pumping gas and fixing cars was no longer fun.

Sonny decided to make the best of this progress and proceeded to mount components of his gasoline station livelihood onto a trailer. The way he saw it, a mobile "petroliana" museum that toured the states could feature those long-lost qualities of full service and show the public just what they were missing.

He was right on the mark! Audience members who see the show become so involved by the story that they see Reehl as the real McCoy—an actual service station attendant ready to answer questions about car care and engines. He's that and more, combining five former employers into one gas pump personality.

At the end of the show, those in attendance come to recall the forgotten ways of the classic American gas station, including the values of customer service and the pursuit of quality. For Reehl, that revelation is what makes all the work and dedication worth it. For him, Sonny the gas station attendant is one of the most satisfying roles he has ever had the opportunity to play.

So don't even bother looking between the rows and rows of chrome-plated pumps for the classic service station attendant of old. He's outmoded now; an extinct species that has no place at today's station. On occasion you may find him on the backroads, in small towns, and at the edge of forgotten roadsides where time has stopped. If you do, make sure he checks under the hood, wipes your windows, and gives you a handful of Green Stamps. Fill 'er up! Pay in cash and tip your hat, for the next time you pass, it's likely that he and his station will be gone.

Gas station attendants were once required to wear head attire such as this. Fifty years ago, long distance travel was still a big deal and the station man was viewed as a professional—one that enabled the motorist to get from one place to another with the utmost in speed and safety. ©2000 Coolstock.com

The house-style gas station was quite popular for many brands of gasoline. It was the perfect format to conjure up positive associations in the mind of the motorist. *Courtesy Phillips Petroleum Company*

Because there were no gasoline gauges in the early motorcars, a wooden dipstick with graduated markings served as a rudimentary fuel gauge. It allowed even the most unskilled operator to quickly level a tank without overflow.

As it happened, there was so much excitement about the *idea* of the drive-up filling station, that little thought was given to the station architecture itself. All creative energies went into perfecting the carefree refueling concept that Laessig and Grenner had started. The machine known as the gasoline pump was the focus for innovation and the epicenter of station evolution. The timing wasn't right at this point because no one had made a fuss about station appearance yet.

However, the first architectural inroads toward gas station design were being made vis-à-vis the gasoline pump. Just like a column, post, or pillar, a gas pump added a certain ambiance to a building. Owners could enhance the public perception of their enterprise by planting a gas pump along the curbside. It didn't matter if you ran a general store, post office, or blacksmith shop. The pump was the accessory that moved your structure to a new level. Being equipped with one or more pumps, advertised that you were a gas station and by all appearances, were friendly to the motoring hobby.

The movement toward stately gas stations reached its peak during the 1930s. Stations such as this Gulf example showed how the lowly gas station could hold its own with the elaborate architecture of banks and city halls. *Photograph provided, and reprinted with permission, by Chevron Corporation*

Historical photographs and company records make it clear that the majority of America's first gas stations were hybrid businesses. A combination of merchandise store (or other business) and gasoline depot, they had a lot in common with the total merchandising gas stations that populate today's roadsides. Gas and oil were simply commodities added to the inventory list.

But that fact was soon to change. As the 1910s and 1920s ushered in a frenzied climate for the purchase of automobiles, oil companies made it just as easy for entrepreneurs to get into the retail gas business. Independent operators interested in making a fast buck signed a contract with a petroleum company

real "drive-up" service station on the corner of Baum Boulevard and St. Clair in Pittsburgh, Pennsylvania. Designed solely for serving automobiles, the hexagonal building allowed customers to drive up for gasoline on all sides. Under an overhanging roof, pumps installed around the station hut serviced the cars that drove in.

While others may have been first in servicing cars with filler hoses or other such contrivances, the Gulf operation was unique. It was a refueling operation that served no purpose other than selling gas and oil products. Station attendants were single-minded in their duties—they scurried about and filled up the vehicles, sold some motor oil when they could, and made sure that the customers were served well. Plain and simple, it was all related to gasoline. Here, there was no gingham fabric to measure, no potatoes to weigh, nor penny candy to dole out.

Gulf's gasoline station format was obviously superior, and it didn't take long for the general concept to catch on with all the major players in the oil refining business. By the decade's end, a nationwide campaign was underway to standardize stations. If a motorist visited a station in Santa Monica, California, and then motored to Chicago, Illinois, via Route 66, all of the gasoline depots encountered along the way would look the same. Moreover, they would feature

continued on page 116

Mobil embarked on a plan to retail tires, batteries, and accessories by designing a station with an expansive sales window. The famous, streamlined, oil drum design shown in this image created a great feeling of architectural balance. Note the porthole window to the left. *Courtesy A. J. Vogel*

Throw up a canopy and attach it to the front of your general store and what do you have? A gas station with a weatherproof area for filling cars. This station was located near Lignum, Virginia. ©2000 Coolstock.com

on Monday, nailed together a shack on Tuesday, and installed some pumping equipment on Wednesday. By the end of the week, they were in business, adding yet another filling station to the roster of streetside locations where motorists could buy fuel.

During the early 1920s, government statistics showed that there were about 15,000 gasoline stations in operation. But the image of the tidy gas station was in the minority. The general consensus was that people were buying gas for their cars, so why construct an expensive hut simply to house a station attendant? The purchase of pumps and installation of underground fuel tanks was enough of an expense for the early station proprietors. A customized structure intended solely for the pumping of fuel into an empty gasoline tank seemed a frivolous expense.

Nevertheless, some semblance of progress was being made towards the gentrification of the American gas station. In 1913 Gulf Oil pioneered the first

This style of service building was replicated with many variations. The central theme was based on an office, an overhanging canopy, and no garage bays. *National Archives*

111

The general store indicative of small-town America, usually situated somewhere on Main Street, was a style often seen by the traveling motorist. ©*2000 Coolstock.com*

J. E. Hamblen ran this general store and Mobilgas station in Town Hill, Maine. By the size of the sign and the prominence of the pumps, it appears that the business of selling gasoline took over this operation many years ago. *Courtesy Coolstock.com*

Architect Frederick Frost was the genius behind this prototype Mobil station; a multi-pump design featuring the facade of a house and the popular box styling. Only one service bay was included in this design. *Rendering by Donald Dodge, Courtesy Frederick G. Frost, Jr.*

THE BOMBER GAS STATION

In 1947, Art Lacey opened a small, five-pump filling station along Highway 99E in Milwaukie, Oregon. That same year he had his biggest—and his best—idea: Why not mount a full-sized, four-engine airplane on top of his roadside gas station business?

When he heard that the military was scrapping a few World War II leftovers that never saw active duty, he hightailed it to Oklahoma's Altus Air Force Base to check out the grounded surplus. There, he laid eyes on the three-dimensional billboard he was dreaming of—a Lockheed B-29 Superfortress. When he learned just how much it was going to cost, he opted for economy. At the "bargain basement" price of $13,750, the slightly smaller (and just as impressive) B-17 model was really a much better buy.

With the assistance of some local farm boys, the craft was unpickled and readied for the journey home. There was only one problem: Lacey didn't have a pilot's license. During the war, he was an engineer and had garnered only eight hours flying time in a single-engine craft. Nevertheless, the reward of perching a full-sized bomber on top of a gas station was too great to let formalities tie him down. Lacey would take the controls anyway.

Still, there were regulations to satisfy, so he plopped a flight cap on a mannequin and strapped it into the co-pilot's seat! Despite the reckless bravado, his first test flight proved unsuccessful and ended in what some would call a "wheels up" crash. His second airplane was a loss as well—totally trashed in a balls-out belly landing. Fortunately, both

were written off to "wind damage" and a third ship was prepared for flight. With a little luck and a lot of prayers, it proved to be the charm.

This time, Lacey took a few extra precautions along with him: two pilot friends (real ones). The troupe got underway without a hitch, but had a few harrowing encounters en route. A blizzard over the Sierra Nevadas was the worst, equaled only by missing the mountains by mere inches. At one point, the team was so lost that they had to buzz a town in order to read the street signs. It was all a grand adventure, something Lacey reveled in.

Amazingly, they somehow managed to make it to Troutdale, Oregon, in one piece. There, the last leg of the trip proved to be the most difficult. No one would issue a permit to move the plane across town. It was just too big and regulations forbade it. No problem for Lacey. Having come too far to give up his grand plan, Lacey simply strapped the monstrosity on top of four trucks and rolled it to the station site. Of course, the cops were watching and the oversize load earned him a $10 fine. Compared to the future income produced by the station, the amount was laughable.

In the decades that followed, the Bomber annihilated the nearby gas station competition and grew to become one of the nation's premiere refueling attractions. At the height of its glory, its wings shielded a phalanx of 48 computerized pumps and they churned out motor fuel at the rate of 5 million gallons per year. Lacey made a fortune.

Art Lacey came up with the idea of the Bomber Gas Station; an Oregon roadside attraction that continues to grab its share of attention.
Courtesy Jayson Scott, the Bomber Gas Station

Eventually, even the Bomber ran out of airspace. On June 6, 1991, its flight plan was canceled. Faced with a new wave of competition from quickie gas markets and a whopping cost of $250,000 to replace the underground storage tanks, Art Lacey decided to turn in his wings. The famous "bomber complex" would continue to serve with its motel and dining facilities, but the petroleum pumping operation made famous by its stationary B-17 Flying Fortress was closing its bomb bay doors for good.

Today, Lacey's grandson, Jayson Scott, hopes to restore the old airplane to its former splendor. He's formed a non-profit organization (The Bomber Foundation, 13515 S.E. McLoughlin Blvd., Milwaukie, Oregon, 97222) to preserve the plane and estimates that it will cost him at least $1 million to bring the old warbird up to specs. Additional plans are in the works to build a multi-faceted community center to house the vintage flyer and preserve it for coming generations.

If the restoration goes as planned, Art Lacey's Bomber will fly high once again—brightening the gasoline pumpin' skies well into the next millennium. And that is a good thing, for when it comes to gasoline stations that pop out your peepers, Art Lacey's Bomber is a true American original—a prime example of what hard work, luck, and a little bit of imagination can do.

MACHINES FOR REFRESHMENT

From the beginning, selling gasoline and soft drinks was a match made in heaven. In fact, bottled soda pop was probably the first product that filling stations stocked as a sideline, along with oil and car care products. Since drinks such as Coca-Cola and Dr. Pepper were promoted as quick pick-me-up energy drinks, what better way to keep the motorist's mind alert than a bottle of frosty pop?

And so, America's first gas stations, general stores, and mercantile shops stocked cold drinks in any container they could find. Wooden barrels, washtubs, and old buckets provided station owners a ready source for point-of-purchase displays. There was no need for electricity, as refrigeration was yet to be invented. In those days, bulk "refrigerant" arrived in the form of a large frozen block. It was delivered by the iceman himself, riding in a horsedrawn ice wagon, of all things. The chunk was chipped into pieces and spread over the glass bottles to chill them.

A few early pioneers furthered the cause of station soda pop sales by sawing wooden barrels in half and turning the pieces on their side. Legs were attached, creating waist-level cabinets for easy merchandising. To promote a particular brand of soda, attendants nailed the signs that were provided by bottlers to the front of the display case. Concurrently, many built makeshift coolers from shipping crates and bottle cases and positioned them right between the pumps, where motorists could see them. "Gimme a bottle of soda" became as familiar a saying as "Fill 'er up!"

Unfortunately, filling station attendants soon realized that they were spending far too much time dispensing drinks. It would be less distracting and more profitable if customers could help themselves. What the gas stations needed was a self-contained, mechanical vending machine, a unit that combined the properties of a storage cabinet, cooler, and coin collector in one rugged cabinet. Such a device would be as equally handy as a gas pump.

As it happened, the bottling industry was already working on making such a machine a reality. By the mid-1920s, a number of specialized coolers appeared on the market. The first unit to get any serious consideration was a unit called the "Icy-O." It was a small tabletop gadget that resembled a washing tub. Drink buyers turned a top-mounted crank and viewed the bottles inside. The interior rotating "drum" was divided into quarters and was kept cold by filling it up with fragments of ice and water.

Progress in the vending field was swift. In 1928, Coca-Cola engineer John Staton unveiled a rugged cooler that was affordable and versatile. To inhibit rust, the interior box was galvanized, as were all exterior nuts and bolts. Hinged at the center, two metal panels with handles comprised the lid (lending a unique butterfly look). It was the most portable cooler to date, one that came from the factory with swiveling casters on its legs.

The new cooler debuted at the 1929 bottler's convention. Red Coca-Cola signs were affixed to all four sides. The words "Serve Yourself" and "Please Pay the Clerk" were painted on both front and rear panels, respectively. Beneath the storage bin, a shelf allowed dealers to store four yellow Coca-Cola crates full of bottles. With an affordable wholesale price of only $12.50, this unique cooler exceeded sales of 30,000 units the first year.

By 1930, a mechanically refrigerated version of the Glasscock unit

debuted. As refrigeration became a practical concern, most manufacturers refitted their existing coolers to accommodate the technology. When a coin-operated mechanism came on the scene in 1932, the era of the soft drink vending machine had officially begun. Suddenly, the silent salesman of soda pop was dispensing carbonated commodities at filling stations across the land.

Over the next two decades, soda pop vending machines were transformed into works of art. The aesthetics of the soft drink dispenser reached its zenith during the 1950s, when industrial designers copied the streamlining of the automobile. Suddenly, beverage machines sported curvaceous cabinetry, nickel plating, polished brightwork, and high-gloss paint. Artkraft, Cavalier, Mills, Vendo, Vendorlater, Westinghouse, and Quikold offered a variety of attractive coolers to the gas station market.

By the end of the 1950s, the soda machine joined the gas pump as an icon of the gas station. Filling up your gasoline tank and chug-a-lugging an ice cold drink became an important part of the motoring ritual. More often than not, a trip to the gas station meant dropping a nickel into a slot, raising up a cooler lid, and guiding a frosty bottle through the tracks until it was freed. Next to your first kiss and learning how to ride a bike, nothing could compare to popping the top of an icy bottle of soda on a hot summer's day and downing it in one, long, blissful gulp!

The Wayne 60 clockface gas pump is a favorite among gas station collectors, otherwise known as petroliana enthusiasts. Its architectural styling defines the pinnacle of gas pump styling. ©2000 Coolstock.com

Along with the general store, cabin court, and diner, the feed store was a place where many motorists in the country could find a gas pump. ©2000 Coolstock.com

stations. As reported in magazines such as *National Petroleum News*, the gas station was now an "architectural asset." Block by block, it was infiltrating every streetcorner in America.

But the domestic house format and the City Beautiful designs weren't the only games in town. Despite the domestic friendliness of one and stateliness of the other, neither of the styles endured to dominate the gas station industry. While America's mainstream refiners battled it out in the effort to develop the perfect gas station format, a handful of visionaries decided to exploit a completely different angle. For this crowd of non-conformists, the answer to car-owner, consumer appeal on a larger-than-life scale was an architectural form known as "programmatic."

The premise? By combining both the gas station building and the advertising billboard into a single show-stopping structure, gasoline sellers could not only enhance their roadside presence, but heighten the consumer's excitement. At the heart of it all were the crazy constructions designed to make the motorist's eyes bulge, do a double-take, and exclaim, "What the heck was that?"

And so, what began during the giddy days of the 1920s spread across the nation with gleeful abandon. While some gas stations were busy standardizing the image, others were setting themselves apart from the crowd. Like Jazz, the architectural improvisation of programmatic design got people jumping. By the decade's end, fantasy fueling facades of every description festooned the roads.

One of the most recognized models for the gasoline station was borrowed from the everyday machinery used in refueling: the gasoline dispenser. In Maryville, Missouri, out on Highway 71, an independent distributor of Cut Rate gasoline erected a larger-than-life facsimile of the widely used Wayne 60 pumping unit. Inventor Ross McCoy dubbed it the "Big Pump Service Station" and watched the customers roll in.

It was an appropriate name, since the oversized pump shack was just about three-stories high. The station's catchy slogan "Buy Gas Now!" was painted where the calculator numerals normally appeared. Underneath, a large multi-paned picture window with a retractable awning faced out toward traffic.

McCoy completed the unusual layout by installing a pair of life-sized Wayne pumps and a pair of visible register unit dispensers on each side of the unconventional station building. For the automobile customers speeding past, there was little doubt as to what was sold here.

Some of the more eccentric programmatic gas stations took to the skies with an aeronautical motif, riding on the wings of the early craze for flying machines and those daring young aviators who pushed the envelope of pop culture stardom. When one of the early Ford tri-motor airliners touched down in rural Maryville, Tennessee, during the 1920s, brothers Elmer and Henry Nickle were so impressed with the sight that they decided to fashion their new gas station after the state-of-the-art sky bus. Their single-prop "Airplane Service Station" became a much-recognized landmark along the old Clinton Highway and a curiosity magnet that has managed to survive the onslaught of the digital age.

While many rural locations reaped the benefits of amazing architecture, urban areas picked up on the passion as well. Los Angeles was a hotbed of activity for mimetic building styles during the 1930s, typified by Bob's Air Mail Service, an out-of-the-ordinary refueling enterprise located at 5453 Wilshire Boulevard. The twin-prop at Bob's was an actual passenger plane!

Parked as if it had just landed in the driveway, it served motorists with General Petroleum product from gas pumps positioned beneath its wings. A garage structure at the back of the lot was used to repair cars and perform lubrication services. Dubbed "The Happy Landing," the large aluminum craft grabbed the attention of passing customers with its bright colors and Flying Red Horse.

After World War II, the availability of left-over military aircraft and the boom in streetside commerce introduced a new wrinkle to the airplane idea. Engineer, aviator, visionary, and service station showman Art Lacey proved he had the "right stuff" when he piloted a surplus B-17 bomber from Oklahoma's Altus Air Force Base to Troutdale, Oregon. With an idea to use the bird as an "advertising stunt," he paid $13,750 for the Flying Fortress. With a mannequin as co-pilot, Lacey crash-landed two planes before he managed to get a third to its destination and onto its

These days, the remaining stations often serve for the most unusual purposes. One of the most common conversions was the house—the kind that one lives in! *©2000 Coolstock.com*

Unless a gas station building finds another use as a car lot or other business, its days are numbered regardless of the cries issued by preservationists. ©*2000 Coolstock.com*

LOWER DELLS FILLING STATION, WISCONSIN DELLS, WIS.

The Lower Dells Filling Station in Wisconsin Dells, Wisconsin, was perhaps one of the most beautiful Phillips 66 gas stations ever built. With a streamlined building design, a rooftop pylon gushing with glowing light, and fancy Wayne pumps, it was a beacon for motorists at night. *Courtesy Coolstock.com*

Davies, Florida, is the former home of Walter Mears' popular gas station. Throughout its history, the station has appeared in a wide range of architectural styles; the final form taking on a western motif. Alas, the road out front was widened and this station is no longer a reality. ©*2000 Coolstock.com*

This Arizona station exhibits the grand styling seen by many of America's motorists. During the 1950s, the neon clock situated above the entryway became a virtual standard.
©2000 Coolstock.com

CHINN'S CAVE HOUSE
BROOKLYN BRIDGE, KENTUCKY

A gas station in a cave? Why not! Chinn's Cave House in Brooklyn Bridge, Kentucky, did what no other gas station of its day could do. Here is the ultimate in unusual gas station architecture, if you could call it that. *Courtesy Coolstock.com*

final perch atop his gas depot. Fortunately, the majority of prospective gas station owners hoping to boost business didn't have to be so daring. During the 1930s, the notion of selling cut-rate gasoline directly from the railroad tank car to the public caught on—big time. With these trackside sellers, there was no middle man and the motorist could save real money. To promote the concept, the independent known as Premier erected a number of stations that featured elevated tanks at each side of a small house structure. Another gas jobber made up a station house that looked like a railroad tanker. A portion of the "tank" was cut out, creating a canopy for two gas pumps.

While some proprietors were building refueling businesses to copy the appearance of railroad tankers, a few built their station huts to mimic much smaller containers. In 1922, one of these gas station visionaries got the notion to model a station office after a teapot. There was a method to the madness, because the Teapot Dome Service Station was built as a protest against the infamous Teapot Dome oil scandal. (In 1921, President Harding's interior secretary went to prison after a Senate investigation found out that he had leased naval oil reserves at Teapot Dome, Wyoming, and Elk Hills, California, to a pair of speculators who loaned him a large amount of money.) Located on the roadside shelf between Highway 82 and the Yakima Valley Highway (it was moved there in 1984 to make way for the interstate), modern-day travelers may still visit this gasoline jewel just outside of Zillah, Washington.

Today, the quaint shack that began as a way to lampoon political corruption is listed on the National Register of Historic Places. What's more, it's recognized as the oldest surviving, working gasoline station in the United States.

As you might expect, the range of programmatic architecture didn't end with airplanes, railroad cars, and teapots. Equally illuminating to those motorists searching the roadsides for gas, oil, and water were the numerous filling stations fashioned after the familiar form of a lighthouse. It was a great idea, since the ocean-going vessel had much in common with the automobile. Seamen searched for safe harbor and motorists needed a port to replenish their vehicle. Despite the legal registration of the idea, a number of oil marketers went full steam ahead and capitalized on the lighthouse concept. Near Cunningham, Kansas,

The airplane has been a common theme in the history of unusual gas station architecture. This monstrous example took the idea to the outer limits. ©2000 Mike Wallen, courtesy Kent Bash

The Red Apple is a ripe example of the programmatic style of architecture that was popular during the 1920s. Here, car customers could fill their tank with gas, have a cold root beer at the stand, or go inside the apple to consume a sit-down meal. Sandwiches were ten cents! Courtesy Wichita Public Library

In Zillah, Washington, the Teapot
Dome station still stops traffic with
its unconventional architecture.
©2000 Coolstock.com

one reluctant farmer by the name of W.S. "Pat" Grier gained regional notoriety in 1931 when he built the Cairo Lighthouse Service Station on U.S. 54. According to newspaper reports, his wife Hazel is credited with the original design as well as some of the labor. "My mother was pregnant with me when she shingled the top," recalls Jack Grier, her son.

The white-stuccoed lighthouse had many amenities, including a vestibule for the sale of auto parts, a candy counter, a soda pop machine, and even a kerosene stove. The Griers installed a spiral staircase that led up to the second floor, a level that held a special water tank that was used to flush the outhouse toilet out back (flush toilets were a really big deal during the 1930s). A ladder was used to climb into the dome, but there was no light.

In the United States, lighthouses like the one in Kansas became exceedingly popular. By the end of the 1940s, there were a number of tapered beacon stations scattered nationwide. With gas outlets located throughout New York state, The Colonial Beacon Gas Company became the most visible lighthouse chain. Gulf tried its luck with the format, too, and built history's most beautiful lighthouse station in Miami Beach, Florida. A safe haven for motorists who traveled the road along the scenic Intracoastal Waterway, it was billed by Gulf as "the swankiest station in the world!" This was not just hyperbole—the combo of Streamline Moderne architecture and programmatic kitsch made it a decidedly attractive reveler.

But when it came to way-out gas station designs, stucco and steel weren't the only gas station building materials. Wood was a common construction material, especially when you housed your station right inside of a giant tree stump. That's precisely what Bob Ford and Alfred Weger did in 1936, when they opened the "World's Largest Redwood Tree Service Station" on the old path of the 101 Highway leading into Ukiah, California.

For just $25, they purchased an 18-foot section of an old-growth Redwood, hollowed-out the interior, had it cut into slabs, and trucked it out to the site. There, the immense "stump" was reassembled, secured together with cables, and made into a quaint little station office. They slapped a roof on top, added a drive-thru canopy and a few gasoline pumps, and were in business.

Of course, not everyone had gigantic redwood logs to work with. Some gas stations—like the one that was part of the Log City Camp near Carthage, Missouri—used the standard-sized trunks of trees as a material to

THE WIGWAMS, FREE MUSEUM, ROUTE 17, JASPER, N. Y.

The Wigwams Free Museum and Restaurant took the idea of the teepee to new heights. Instead of just building one large teepee like others did, they chose to design the building around a series of teepees–heightening the effect and turning the structure into one big billboard. Note the gas pump display case positioned out on the service island. *Courtesy Coolstock.com*

Located in Weyauwega, Wisconsin, the Wigwam Service Station on Highway 10 wowed motorists with its daring architecture. In regards to building style, the wigwam was unequaled when it came to popping the eyeballs of motorists. *Courtesy Coolstock.com*

PETRIFIED WOOD STATION

10366

The petrified wood station in Lamar, Colorado, was dubbed by W. G. Brown as the "Only Petrified Filling Station in the World." Here is the classic example of American architectural ingenuity at its finest. *Courtesy Coolstock.com*

construct stations. In contrast to store-bought building materials, logs provided a cost-effective way for many of the would-be gasoline, food, and lodging entrepreneurs to get a roadside business started. During the days when the idea of the "West" was enough to stir up the imagination of the motorist, just the sight of a log cabin was enough to pique one's curiosity.

Other gas station builders took the idea of using wood to the ultimate level, using only the fossilized version of the building material. W.G. Brown built one of America's most memorable sites during the 1930s and billed it as the "Only Petrified Wood Filling Station in the World." Filling the tanks of motorists in Lamar, Colorado, Brown's Phillips 66 gas station was definitely striking. It featured a front facade crafted entirely out of petrified logs and gave the impression that the station was carved out of a cave.

Yet, wood (fossilized or not) had its limitations. Back in the 1930s, the Rio Pecos Oil Company of New Mexico proved that point when they built a Route 66 refueler that looked like a giant iceberg selling Cosden gas. Made of plaster and lath, it was a sight that popped out from the roadside landscape and turned heads. Even those hurried motorists speeding by in an automobile couldn't resist.

Some stations such as the legendary "Hat and Boots" in Seattle, Washington, played out stereotypes of the Old West for full effect. With a wide-brimmed Stetson as a roof covering and a pair of larger-than-life cowboy kickers as restroom shacks, the Hat and Boots assured itself a permanent place in the American Roadside Hall of Fame. Believe it or not, the structure still exists and present-day proponents of roadside kitsch are doing what they can to save the monument. Who says roadside kitsch is dead?

Windmills have often been used to market gasoline and oil. This closed station in Washington State lured customers from the roadway with its whimsical appeal. ©*2000 Coolstock.com*

WINDOW TRAVEL DECALS

Remember those cross-country trips in the family automobile and all those station wagons you saw on the highway with tacky tourist decals plastered on their windows? You know, the kind that Dad picked up at the gas stations along the way? Well, those colorful icons of American travel are back and they are showing up at flea markets, collectibles shows, ephemera events, and other well-known gatherings in the world of automobilia.

Once upon a time during the 1940s, 1950s, and 1960s, long before the children of America realized what endless fun can be had by playing with adhesive "stickers," window decals were all the rage. During their travels, Mom and Dad liked to pick them up at tourist traps, motels, gasoline stations, and every other imaginable roadside attraction of importance. They were fun, and told others of all the places and sights that were seen.

The most brag-worthy of favorite destinations included Meremec Caverns along the Ozark region of Route 66, and the Grand Canyon in Arizona. Other decals promoted particular brands of gasoline, tourist accommodations, and service businesses of similar ilk. The most common decals were designed in the shape of a particular state and featured important points of interest within the borders.

Of course, Native American trading posts and tourist attractions, as well as locations where Native Americans once lived were a favorite subject. The state of Delaware produced a stately rendition of a Native American chief—complete with beaded necklace, pigtails, and feather. The Wisconsin Dells region came out with a colorful window decal that took the warrior idea to the next level, showing a chief in full battle dress, complete with feathered headdress and hand-held shield. However,

Bowlin's Running Indian store in New Mexico wasn't as flattering when it came to window decals—its comical version showed a smiling, running brave wielding a tomahawk—pointing his finger at coming attractions.

During their heyday, it was common to see all kinds of humorous travel stickers. Funny sayings such as "I Got my Kicks on Route 66" and "I Got Gassed at Good Gas" were common. For the time, the window decal was the equivalent of today's T-shirt. If you could think of an irreverent slogan or nasty one-liner, it was probably made into a window decal. Of course, the decals of motoring's golden age were seldom crass or obscene (if you don't take into account the regional and racial stereotypes).

With their intense color, highly stylized graphical motifs, and nostalgic themes, these whimsical window decals, born of America's automotive tourist age, are excellent examples of the artistic techniques once used by commercial advertisers. They speak of a time when traveling across the country was really an adventure and the ride was more important than the destination.

Some might ask how to collect decals when most are stuck to the windows of cars that are probably scrap metal by now. The answer is simple. Over the past decade, decals have surfaced at all of the major swap meets and collector gatherings. A fair number of these traveling icons have survived—buried in the bottom of Dad's drawer or hidden away somewhere in a shoebox. Because some motorists never got around to sticking them to the window of the family car, they remain in pristine condition.

For those that like to collect the artifacts now labeled as automobilia, this forgetfulness is a boon. Today, those that are so inclined may pick up fine examples of these water application decals—in excellent shape—

for less than $10. Often, the decals found are in mint condition and stored in the original glassine envelope that they were originally sold in—complete with detailed instructions on how to apply them to a window.

When arranged in a plastic-page display book, mounted in a framed series, or blown up with a color copier for individual display, these compact examples of retro-tourism are a great addition to any collector's exhibit area. For those with classic cars, it's extremely tempting to actually use some of these decals—and many do. Along with those decals of the hot rod and speed equipment variety, tourist-type appliqués can provide just the right touch to make a classic ride look "original."

Considering the appealing nature and general rarity, one would think that window decals are in big demand. Not so. A few ardent fans are just beginning to appreciate their beauty, while the bulk of decal collectors clamor over the racing-style decals.

For that and the many other reasons listed here, those always colorful travel-type window decals of yesteryear are a great way for the collector to relive those crazy days of two-lane travel and tourist traps. The only trouble in collecting them is trying to resist the great temptation to slap them on the family station wagon, crank up the car radio, and hit the road!

Along with the cowboy stations came the stations associated with Native American culture. In Browning, Montana, Kramer's Wigwam stopped traffic by serving motor fuel and people fuel (sandwiches) from a two-story representation of a teepee. Outfitted with four visible-register gasoline pumps and all the standard equipment, it was a popular haven for tired tourists and the occasional motorist, who required a new set of General tires.

Geronimo's Castle in Bowie, Arizona, sold refinery products as well, but it paled in comparison to the folkish chain of gasoline station/restaurants conceived by Frank Redford in 1933. After he constructed his first prototype in Horse Cave, Kentucky, it didn't take long for the concept to stampede its way across the

country. With the later addition of teepee-shaped motel units, the Wigwam Village chain became a favorite overnight resting stop in seven states. Neon signs entreating motorists to "Eat and Sleep in a Wigwam" lit up the American night and the imaginations of road-weary travelers. Travelers could fill their tanks at the wigwam, as well.

Unfortunately, all good things must come to an end, and so it was with the eccentric architecture of the gas station. In spite of their overwhelming success, mimetic refueling structures fell out of favor. With the advent of radio, then television, petroleum refiners found it easier to get their names out over the airwaves.

Gradually, as automobiles began to speed down the superhighways of the future, the unsophisticated

attractions once regarded as "entertaining" lost their luster. The car owner of the twentieth century—his or her senses jaded by skyscrapers, bridges, and other feats of engineering—began to view the remaining programmatic-themed gasoline stations as marketing traps.

With that, the architecture of the American gasoline station changed. It was the 1950s and the desire to market all sorts of products moved to the forefront. In the name of boosting average sales and profits, refiners remade the gasoline station service facility into the image of total merchandising. Large plate glass windows and a separate office allowed the station owner to conduct his business in one place and sell goods at the same time.

In industry magazine articles and pamphlets, design experts espoused theories about how to best lay-out a station floor plan, how to plan traffic flow, and where to plant the shrubbery. Running a station was no longer a simple matter, but a science.

Today, the memory of yesterday's fantastic filling stations grows dim. An adherence to conformity haunts the motorways with a pervading banality. Now, the gasoline station is simply a utility and a place for people to get more gas. Gone are the "way-out" wonders—the weird, the wacky, and the whimsical! Exaggerated architecture is no longer welcome and it can be said that the heyday of crazy roadside creations is over. And for that, we can all shed a quiet tear while we pump our own gas in the self-service lane.

The Gas and Boots station of Seattle, Washington, is perhaps the most striking example of gas station architecture still in existence. The hat served as the office and the boots as the restrooms. ©2000 Coolstock.com

Chapter 5

THE NEW ERA OF AMERICAN GASOLINE

POWERING AUTOMOBILES FOR THE FUTURE

$ 002.00 DOLLARS

00 1.600 GALLONS

PRICE PER GALLON INCLUDING TAX

REGULAR 1.209

UNLEADED 1.249 ←

PREMIUM 1.269

The American gasoline station is changing. Can you remember the last time a service station attendant pumped gasoline into your automobile, cleaned your windshield, or looked under the hood? The fact is, there are very few full-service gasoline stations left. For better or worse, self-service has become the rule of the roadways. Most motorists have accepted the "convenience" and barely noticed the transition.

Did you ever stop to wonder why there are so few mom-and-pop gas stations left? Part of the answer lies with the Environmental Protection Agency (EPA); a governmental agency entrusted with the care and well-being of our environment. In 1998, the EPA issued a decree that all aging underground gas tanks be replaced within a period of 10 years. Of the nation's one million gas tanks, a minority were leaking and contaminating ground water. Big or small, it didn't matter. All gas stations were required to meet the new guidelines in the specified amount of time.

This was a major expense, as the typical station had as many as three to four tanks buried underground. The cost to dig up the tanks and install new ones could run as high as $100,000. Of course, this was less of a burden for the major oil corporations—the stations that were no longer profitable were shut down and the still-thriving gas stations were enhanced. Meanwhile, mom-and-pop businesses wondered how they were going to borrow the money to replace their tanks.

The 10 years passed quickly, and in 1998, the deadline date to replace the tanks came and went. News sources estimated that some 20,000 stations were likely to fail compliance and face shutdown. The EPA wasn't going to show leniency either. Agency spokeswoman Tanya Meekins sealed the fate of all the station owners who were worried about their tanks: "Ten years is long enough," she said. "Even if they have a contractor signed up to do the work, that's not good enough. It must be done by the deadline."

Stations who hadn't replaced their tanks in time had to shut off the pumps and stop selling gas, or face fines of up to $11,000 a day. It didn't take a rocket scientist to see what was going on. The small businessman was holding the short end of the stick and the large companies had the advantage. Faced with this enormous expense—one that was often more than the entire value of their station, many gas stations simply pumped their tanks dry and closed down. The ranks of the small, independent gas station were decimated and a part of recent American history was lost.

At the same time, remaining gas stations backed away from general automotive repair services. Where only a few short years ago you could find a service station with an open garage bay and mechanic, these types of hybrid businesses have become a rare sight.

All of a sudden, being stranded out on the road with a dead battery or flat tire means having to call a travel association or an independent wrecker

Go with Phillips 66...
the gasoline that won the West!

It's just plain horse sense to stop at Phillips 66. Phillips gasoline gives you more gallop-per-gallon. That's why it's made so many friends in the West.

And when it comes to service, you'll find Phillips mighty big on western hospitality, too. In fact, many of

our stations are equipped to vacuum your car free. All you have to do is ask your friendly Phillips 66 dealer.

No wonder Phillips 66 is making a big name for itself in 49 states. So go first-class ... go Phillips 66. Get the gasoline and the hospitality that won the West!

PHILLIPS 66

Phillips used the mystique of the West in a series of ads that ran during the 1960s. Using cowboys, indians, and horses, they got the point across that Phillips gasoline was the fuel to use when traveling long distances. *Coolstock.com Collection, Courtesy Phillips Petroleum Company*

In many vehicles, just changing the sparkplugs has become a major mechanical project. Do you own a mid-sized vehicle equipped with a transverse-mounted engine? If so, it's often necessary to tilt the engine in order to gain access to the rear plugs! Other cars require you to remove the wheel and take off the entire wheel well in order to gain access to the battery—now that's progress.

It's no wonder the "shade tree" mechanic is dead. Now, the art of auto repair demands top dollar and the skills of a highly trained service mechanic. Only the bigger chain stores and corporate entities can afford the complicated equipment that's required to fix the average auto. Not only have computers invaded the realm of the automobile itself, they have completely changed the nature of diagnostics. Go ahead, toss that old sparkplug gapper and timing light right into the trash bin! If you could afford it, a well-equipped automotive diagnostic repair bay would cost you more than a small suburban house!

Nationwide chain automobile fix-it operations such as Pep Boys, Jiffy Lube, Montgomery Wards, Meineke, Midas, Sears, Firestone, Western Auto, and your local car dealer have usurped the duties once held by the gas station grease monkey. Repairing a car in an emergency, and then getting it back on the road within a few short hours, is no longer a possibility even in the best circumstances. Appointments must be made, loaner cars reserved, and waiting lists assigned. These days, it's best to have one car in reserve for when your car breaks down, or take a taxi.

The nature of today's high-tech vehicles, the lack of mechanic facilities, and the prerequisite for elaborate test equipment has led to many problems "on the road." Long-distance trips must be planned with great care. If you drive an aging vehicle, it must be checked over thoroughly by a technician before you

This Texas Tidex station still strikes a modern pose even though this photograph was taken during the early 1950s! *Courtesy Coolstock.com*

Staying in a log cabin and filling up your car at a gas station like this used to be a real kick. Where else could you get fried chicken and liquor all in the same stop? Today, picture postcards are the only reminder of these truly American roadside haunts. *Courtesy Coolstock.com*

Chrome and graffiti just seem to go together. The handwriting is on the wall (so to speak), and the generation of the gasoline station is nearing its close. The age of solar power is dawning and new possibilities in transportation are upon us. *©2000 Coolstock.com*

leave. The tires must be examined carefully for any leaks, as only temporary use of the space-saving spare tires is recommended. Be sure to carry along a tool kit and service manual in your trunk, too. You may need them if you get stranded out in the boondocks.

Fortunately, other technologies promise to come to the aid of the American automobile owner and lessen the need for traditional roadside services. Car manufacturers are taking full advantage of once-classified military hardware, and linking in-car mapping systems to the constellation of 24 geosynchronous positioning system (GPS) satellites orbiting the Earth. Advances in compact, low-power, and low-cost microprocessors have allowed players like Motorola to supply the industry with cost-effective and practical solutions.

"Telematics" systems, otherwise knows as automotive wireless communication devices, that provide drivers with personalized info, messaging, entertainment, and location-specific travel and security services are revolutionizing motoring. High tech installations such as Nissan's Infiniti Communicator, General Motors' Vauxhall OnStar System, Visteon's Vehicle Emergency Messaging System, Mercedes' TELE AID System, Ford's Lincoln Remote Emergency Satellite Cellular Unit (RESCU) System, and Renault's Telematics System are changing the face of private and commercial transportation.

Cadillac is leading the way with the OnStar system, a popular GPS receiver and cellular telephone combination made famous by TV ads featuring the Batmobile. Owning a vehicle equipped with the

Let us pay homage to the gas pumps of America: gone, but not forgotten. We will miss you and your low prices. ©*2000 Coolstock.com*

Standing as a sentinel off of Highway 35, south of Fort Worth, Texas, this pump stands as a memorial of the past; a grave marker that signifies the passing of an era. ©*2000 Coolstock.com*

OnStar system, the ordinary commuter doesn't have to be a superhero to get help. When you break down, get lost on the road, or are simply looking for roadside services, simply push the OnStar button and a friendly service representative is summoned. In a matter of moments, you will have directions to your destination.

But even this advanced system may soon appear to be redundant. In the coming future, the gas station will be quite easy to find, as the hybrid grocery supply outlet and refueling depot will be situated on almost every street corner. Economics has caused the gas station proprietor to go back to the past and rediscover the ways of our

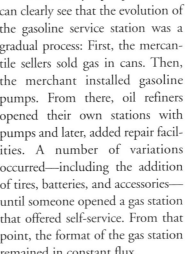

roadside ancestors. The gasoline station has come full circle. Once again, the general store and sundry supply is part of the equation.

From today's perspective, we can clearly see that the evolution of the gasoline service station was a gradual process: First, the mercantile sellers sold gas in cans. Then, the merchant installed gasoline pumps. From there, oil refiners opened their own stations with pumps and later, added repair facilities. A number of variations occurred—including the addition of tires, batteries, and accessories—until someone opened a gas station that offered self-service. From that point, the format of the gas station remained in constant flux.

Only remnants of yesterday's gas stations can be found along the superhighways of America. Today, the full-service truck stop with all of the amenities rules the roads. ©2000 Coolstock.com

This Super Shell pump is a friendly reminder of the 1970s; a time when gas prices exploded and lines were long. Will we see another gas crisis in the near future? Only time will tell. ©2000 Coolstock.com

With a plant literally growing up into its front panel, this pump appears to be returning to nature. Someday, all pumps could be used as planters as the supply of oil is not endless. Gasoline may not be the ultimate fuel source. ©2000 Coolstock.com

Ironically, the merchandising of gasoline has returned to the old ways and the days of the merchant. Modern gasoline stations offer motorists a variety of products, including food, automotive supplies, and travel accessories. Motorists appear to like the format, as a variety of sundries may now be purchased quickly, eliminating the need to visit the local supermarket and negotiate crowded parking lots or wait in long check-out lines. Offering up Cherry Slushes, corn dogs, potato chips, pretzels, soft drinks, and beer—the present day American gas station is definitely not the same service station that your father grew up with!

This return to retail started with the chain store known as 7-Eleven. During the 1970s, the Southland Corporation began to grow their marketing territories in Texas and reintroduced America to the convenient combo of gas and goods. People appreciated the convenience or self-service gas and soon, the idea spread beyond the boundaries of the Southwest. By the end of the decade, there were many 7-Eleven clones, all copying the convenience store concept and taking it nationwide to a receptive audience.

The timing was right for success. With an emphasis placed on speed, boasting a specialized stock of cash-and-carry merchandise, and self-service pumps, convenience stores came to dominate the gasoline retail trade. Despite the limited amenities that were offered in terms of refueling and servicing a car, convenience stores rose to become the dominant force along the roadside. Today, we have many such outlets in all 50 states, doing business under memorable names like Ameristop, Sack and Pack, Quik-Mart, U-Pick-Em, Pick and Pay, E-Z Mart, RaceTrac, Love's, Pilot, U-Tote-Em, and more.

When video game machines made their debut during the 1970s, many of the convenience stores installed machines to boost revenues. Of course, American teenagers came in droves, plunked down

Phillips 66, a venerable gas station brand and a big favorite of petroliana collectors, still attracts the interest of gas pump and oil can aficionados. ©2000 Coolstock.com

Mobilgas: The Flying Red Horse, familiar red pump, and porcelain-enameled sign are all collected today because of their rarity. ©2000 Coolstock.com, Courtesy the General Petroleum Museum

Ashtrays imprinted with oil company logos are a prime collectible in today's circles. Smoking paraphernalia is a major segment of the hobby in which many collectors specialize. ©2000 Coolstock.com

their quarters, and turned the modern general store into the new hangout. In terms of being seen, the convenience store of the 1980s was just as important as the drive-in movie or drive-in restaurant were during the 1950s. Heralded as a new icon for American teen culture, the convenience store was immortalized in several films, including *Clerks.*

These days, video games may be played at home and most of the kids have moved on to more entertaining handouts. Vying for the food and gasoline customers that remain, the competition among convenience retailers is fierce. To pull in the trade and keep it coming back, roadside convenience refuelers are trying all kinds of new gimmicks. Of recent note is the trend towards "co-branding," a novel method of merchandising that combines two recognized brand names under one roof, at one location. For instance, one brand might be famous for their gas and the other for their hamburgers. Customers in a rush can find gasoline and food in one stop.

The stand-alone eatery is becoming an artifact of the past as gasoline and fast-food restaurants merge to form a single entity. Nationally advertised fast-food chains such as Burger King, Pizza Hut, Baskin-Robbins, Dunkin' Donuts, Subway, and Blimpie are

45,000 MOBILGAS DEALERS PROVE A POINT!

A Good Man is <u>Not</u> Hard to Find

Mobilgas
SOCONY-VACUUM

What's a "good man"?

For you, a motorist, he's a man *who knows your car* . . .

He's expert, experienced, courteous.

He delivers quality products—with quality service.

With 45,000 Mobilgas dealers coast-to-coast, you're never very far from him, either.

Backed by the company with 82 years' leadership in Petroleum Progress—with Mobilgas—U.S.A.'s favorite gasoline—Mobiloil—the world's largest-selling motor oil, and the famous Mobil Line of Tires, Batteries, Accessories . . . *He's your man* with everything your car needs—

AT THE SIGN OF FRIENDLY SERVICE

SOCONY-VACUUM OIL COMPANY, INC., and Affiliates: MAGNOLIA PETROLEUM COMPANY, GENERAL PETROLEUM CORPORATION

According to this Mobil ad, a good service station man is not hard to find. Just drive down to your local Mobil dealer and you will find him pumping gas, filling up tires, and lubricating the chassis of cars! *Coolstock.com Collection, Courtesy Mobil Corporation*

CLASSICAL *Gas*

THE AEROPLANE GAS STATION

In 1925, a Ford Motor Company tri-motor airliner landed near Maryville, Tennessee, and made the local headlines. It was the biggest winged craft to ever touch down in this rural area and quickly captured the interest of the locals.

Deeply affected by the visit were Elmer and Henry Nickle. Two brothers with big ideas, they were so taken by the sight of the big bird, and the response of the townspeople, that they decided to fashion their new business after it. The Nickle brothers planned to open a filling station and decided the building should look just like an airplane. Under the circumstances, they believed it would be a perfect way to attract local customers and those passing through.

Around the same time, the new Clinton Highway was being paved over by the county to replace the Old Clinton Pike. With this promise of increased traffic secured, the two brothers soared into action. Aware that their new gasoline building was sure to attract attention, they crafted a scaled-down replica of the big bird and perched it on the side of the highway right where the passing traffic could see it. To provide for the big business to come, they installed three hand-operated gasoline pumps.

The airplane building was a magnet for car customers, who came in great numbers. As the vehicles rolled in, the Nickle brothers were inspired and began to formulate a plan to construct a chain of "aeroplane" service stations. From Cincinnati, Ohio, to Tampa, Florida, eager tourists traveling by car would be drawn in as customers for gasoline, oil, and ice-cold sodas.

Unfortunately, the Nickles' grandiose vision of an East Coast service station chain evaporated into the clouds. With the onset of the Great Depression, stocks were worthless and the money supply was tight. The brothers were barely getting by as it was and there were few investors who were willing to take a risk.

Somehow, Elmer and Henry managed to keep the station flying and by the early 1940s, the automotive business slowly rebounded. When the nearby "atomic city" of Oak Ridge began its tremendous spurt of growth, Elmer left the pumps to work there as a mechanic. Undaunted, brother Henry took the pilot's seat at the gas station and flew the business onward to meet his dreams.

When the Clinton Highway expanded again, this time to handle four lanes of commuter traffic during World War II, his years of patience finally began to reap their reward. On a daily basis, streams of workers cruising by in their automobiles passed the gleaming aeroplane on their way to the factories in town. In the morning and evening, a rush of commuters stopped for service.

Suddenly, there was more business than ever before as workers pulled in to get their tanks filled, oil checked, and windows wiped. To handle the increased business and keep the customers happy, Nickle hired on two additional gas station attendants. With the added help, the aeroplane station remained open between 6:00 A.M. and 8:00 P.M., boosting the take to an average of $200 to $300 in gasoline sales every day!

After years of satisfying car customers, Henry Nickle had his fill of the gasoline business and eventually retired. As the pumps ceased to flow, the aeroplane building was purchased and sold numerous times, and was used for a variety of other purposes. There was something appealing about the look of the place, and to the Nickles' credit, no one could tear it down.

Capitalizing on the craze for flying, the Aeroplane gas station housed its station office inside the fuselage of a mock aircraft. By today's standards it may seem a bit hokey, but decades ago, it was an idea that still turned heads. ©*2000 Jim Caulfield*

At one time, the tapered fuselage housed a compact liquor store. Years later, the silver bird saw service as a bait shop. More recently, the building was utilized as a fruit stand. The last tenant to operate a business from the static flyer was the Clinton Highway Service Center, a used parts emporium that sold parts for recreational vehicles. Regardless of its occupant, this unusual roadside building has evolved into a local landmark.

These days, the airplane building Elmer and Henry Nickle built is unoccupied. Now, the once eye-popping station gets nothing more than a cursory glance. With rocket-powered spacecraft a current reality, the sight of a small roadside airplane no longer inspires attention. Commuters speeding down Pleasant Ridge Road still take note of the sight, but buy their gas elsewhere. Now, a large billboard towers over the structure, diminishing its importance.

Sadly, the Aeroplane Gas Station neither stirs up memories of the biggest airliner "ever seen" nor inspires dreams of the future. Today, it is an architectural oddity of the American roadside; a crumbling reminder of a past forgotten . . . and somehow lost. If Elmer and Henry Nickle had their way, we would still have a chain of aeroplane stations up and down the coast.

The White Eagle gas pump globe is yet another highly sought after item by the petroliana collector. ©2000 Coolstock.com

Driving safely during the heyday of motoring meant keeping it under 50 miles per hour. Now if you can stay in the slow lane of the local freeway while you are doing 70, you can call yourself lucky. ©2000 Coolstock.com

enthusiastically aligning themselves with petroleum refineries. Chevron, Amoco, and Shell are forging an exclusive relationship with McDonalds. Within the next few years, motorists will not be able to make a refueling stop without seeing the familiar logo of their favorite fast-food eatery.

Meanwhile, out on the serving lot, changes are underway to improve the gas pump. One of the most exciting developments to hit the highways is the Gilbarco Eclipse. Manufactured by Marconi Commerce Systems, Inc., this revolutionary fuel dispenser elevates the process of gassing up an automobile to the next level. Using proprietary technology and a computing system enhanced by microprocessors from Motorola, the Eclipse is capable of providing customers a rich experience while they pump their gas. Since Gilbarco's modern fuel dispenser uses basic Web building blocks, retailers have the flexibility of adding Web-based services through the dispenser. Gasoline

Welcome to the machine. In the future, the American gas pump will be ruled by automation and robotics. Maybe someday scientists will craft an animatronic drone of the classic gas station service attendant. ©2000 Coolstock.com

The Black Hills' Largest Outdoor Free Museum, Located 2½ Miles East of Custer, S.D. on US Highway 16.

retailers can configure and control the screen content so that it matches their need for local control, user interface graphics, and price. The built-in InfoScreen eye-level display panel is the main point of focus, transforming the pump into an interactive kiosk.

Today's customers can entertain themselves as they pump their gas. Forget about checking the oil or dragging a dirty squeegee over the windshield. As the fuel flows into the tank, motorists of the new millennium have the option of checking the latest news headlines, scores, or stock prices. Gas stations can even program the unit to display current specials and other forms of advertising to transform the gas pump into a modern day equivalent of the display case pumps of the 1930s.

As part of the new system, a keytag or car-mounted transponder will allow customers to refuel their cars with ease. When you pull up to the Eclipse pump, it will already know what grade of gas you prefer! No need to run inside and pay with cash or even present a debit card to slide in a reader: the new Gilbarco unit debits your credit card account—automatically! Additional options are also available that will allow the pump to integrate a card reader or a cash reader, allowing the station owner unprecedented flexibility.

As it sets the standard for state-of-the-art stations, the Gilbarco unit has raised the bar of the gasoline pump cabinet aesthetic as well: the new unit harkens back to the days of the tall, slender, graceful, visible register pumps. Each slender pump features dual-sided pumping, a high-gloss painted fiberglass skin, and rounded edges.

Marconi's Gilbarco Eclipse is only a glimpse of what the future will hold for the gasoline purchaser! In 1996, *Automobile* magazine reported in "Gas Stations

The Black Hills largest outdoor free museum was located 2.5 miles east of Custer, South Dakota, on U.S. Highway 16. Big agates, polished stones, rare minerals, and deer antlers were the big draw at this tourist trap. *Courtesy Coolstock.com*

155

Out of gas and out of luck, many former mom-and-pop gas stations have found other options. With ample parking space, opening a used car dealership is a perfect alternative. ©2000 Coolstock.com

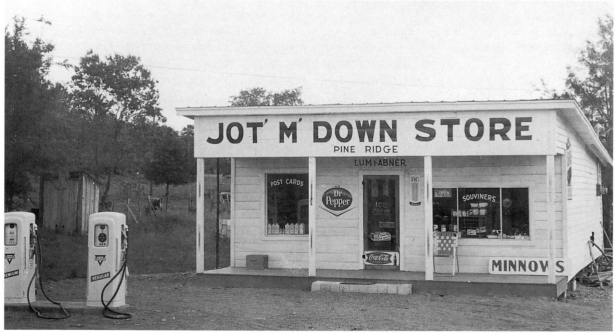

At the Jot 'M' Down store in Pine Ridge, minnows were a big hit, as were the sale of "souvineers." You won't find this kind of merchandise down at the local 7-Eleven!
Courtesy Coolstock.com

Past, Present, and Future" that the Mobil Corporation was experimenting with expanded attendant service. The author predicted that one day, "ghost stations" manned by self-service robots would rule the day. Able to work long hours for no pay, gas station robots would usher in a whole new era of service—albeit sterile and impersonal.

The article proved to be more than mere speculation. Believe it or not, the era of the gasoline station robot has arrived! The Shell Oil Company, already known for its many industry innovations over the course of gasoline history, is paving a wide path to the future with the first automated refueling station on the planet. It's a radically new refueling

technology the company began field-testing in April 1997 with 500 gasoline customers in Sacramento, California. Motorists involved with the test responded so well to the automated pump system that Shell has now rolled out what they call the "SmartPump" to general consumers in one Indiana market. Jerry Buri, project manager for Shell, recently reported that over 1,000 customers have signed up for the SmartPump program.

If one takes into account the respectable roster of high-tech companies that were involved with the development of the new pump setup, motorists will not be disappointed. The pumping components that quickly move fuel from the underground tanks into

At the Sall-Mar Court, Texaco gasoline was sold exclusively. Today, the same sort of co-branding schemes are being worked out by major brands all across the nation. Motels are out, and fast-food restaurants have teamed up with the gas station. *Courtesy Coolstock.com*

SALL-MAR COURT RAPID RIVER, MICH 21398

Off the old Route 66 Highway, this gas station throwback unfortunately returns to nature. ©2000 Coolstock.com

It used to be that you could find a gas station on almost every street corner. Now, that is true only of intersections along major highways. On the outskirts, the number of gas stations are running thin and services are becoming non-existent. ©2000 Coolstock.com

the car were refined by Marconi Commerce Systems (formerly Gilbarco). The special fuel cap that allows a wide range of automobiles to accept the special SmartPump refueling nozzle was designed by the Stant Manufacturing Corporation. International Submarine Engineering of Canada pitched in with motion sensor technology. Texas Instruments provided the technology for the small windshield transponder that activates the system. H.R. Textron—the company that makes motion-control systems for jets, guided missiles, and the animated characters at the Disney theme parks—pulls it all together and manufactures the SmartPump system for Shell.

But the gas customer need not be concerned with the technical aspects of the system. Operation of the SmartPump is simple and convenient: The motorist simply drives up to a predetermined spot in the pumping lane and waits. The unit reads the information from the windshield transponder and learns what kind of car you are driving and which credit card account to charge for your gasoline purchase. A green light signals for the customer to pull ahead to a "customer interface terminal" to select the preferred octane.

With that taken care of, the overhead pump arm automatically swings into position, guided by the make and model info provided by the transponder and kept in check by sensitive probes. The robotic arm locates your filler cap and uses a clever suction cup to pull open the fuel door. Next, the filler nozzle is carefully inserted into your car's spring-loaded refueling cap and the gas begins to flow. The whole process takes about three minutes. When the robot arm retracts to its resting position, the customer is free to hit the road without any further interaction.

SmartPump is limited only when it comes to servicing some of the older makes of cars on the road. Vehicles that have gas caps behind license plates are unserviceable as are custom cars and hot rods with unusual fill configurations. Presently, SmartPump isn't smart enough to pump gas in small increments, so "filling it up" is the only way to go. There's an extra cost involved to use the system, too. Customers must pay an upfront deposit of $20 to use the system and after 90 days, Shell keeps the deposit (if the consumer decides to use the system on a regular basis). After a three month grace period, there is a $1 transaction fee levied each time SmartPump is used.

How will you run that car or motorcycle without refined gasoline? When the oil runs out or prices shoot too high for the average consumer, hitchhiking may be the only alternative left.
©2000 Coolstock.com

MY MOBIL SPEED PASS

When I first applied for my Mobil SpeedPass, I was jazzed about pumpin' fast gas. Just the thought of refueling my car quickly was appealing. With Mobil's window-mounted box or keychain-style transponder, I could beat the clock and cut the hassle. To apply for a SpeedPass, you fill out a postage-paid form and drop it in a mailbox. The SpeedPass account attaches itself to Mobil's own credit card or virtually any other type of credit card. What could be easier?

I ordered two SpeedPasses and gave the extra one to my wife, despite her vocal skepticism. They arrived quickly and were packed in a cardboard container that mocked the luxury of a small jewelry box. Inside, positioned to give the impression of treasure, were two plastic key fobs sporting gleaming chrome rings. Both were black and imprinted with a serial number. It was the sporty racing ribs around the tip that caught my eye, offering an illusion that the SpeedPass emits an extra-special light ray that speeds things up. Similar to something out of a *Star Trek* episode, it just looks cool.

A small sticker in the box alerts you to call and activate the tags, something I did right away. Minutes later, I jumped into the car and raced off to find the nearest station. Those who choose the deck-mounted window unit must park close enough for the pump to scan the box. With the key fob, a deft wave in front of the pump sensor is all that is necessary. Once the chip is scanned, your I.D. code is sent to billing and gasoline flows.

The general idea of the whole system is that while the rest of the low-tech customers cram their antiquated credit cards into debit machines or pay with cash, SpeedPass owners wave their magic wand in front of the pump sensor, top off their tank, and zoom away. Say hello to instant gratification and minimal human interaction, and say goodbye to credit cards and cash!

The Mobil SpeedPass worked just as advertised at my first visit to the pumps as a SpeedPass member. I waved my little black talisman in front of the pump sensor and with a ruddy brilliance, the red "Peggo" flashed to life! I didn't have to insert my credit card or go inside the station. The pump was pumping and all was right with the world.

Even so, I didn't feel quite as cool when I waved the gadget in front of the sensor. Frankly, I felt just a little bit self-conscious. Were my compadres at the pumps watching me, aware of my contempt for their outmoded method of payment? It didn't matter. Satisfied with my prowess at the pumps, I nodded a quick thank you to the Flying Red Horse, snapped off my receipt, and hopped back into the car. I was back on top as the prince of pumps! It was during this moment of serendipity that my car coughed, rolled a few feet, and stalled. It would not restart. Through no fault of Mobil, the oh-so-handy SpeedPass proved to be ineffective when it came to engine trouble. Here was the fastest pumper in the West, stranded on a full tank of gasoline with a bum starter.

For the next hour, I slurped down a Slushee, chewed on some beef jerky, and yakked on my cell phone. The AAA wrecker man was coming and now I had oodles of time to kill. As I sat on the curb waiting, I pondered the benefits of my Mobil SpeedPass and the relativity of time. Perhaps I was trying to save *too* much.

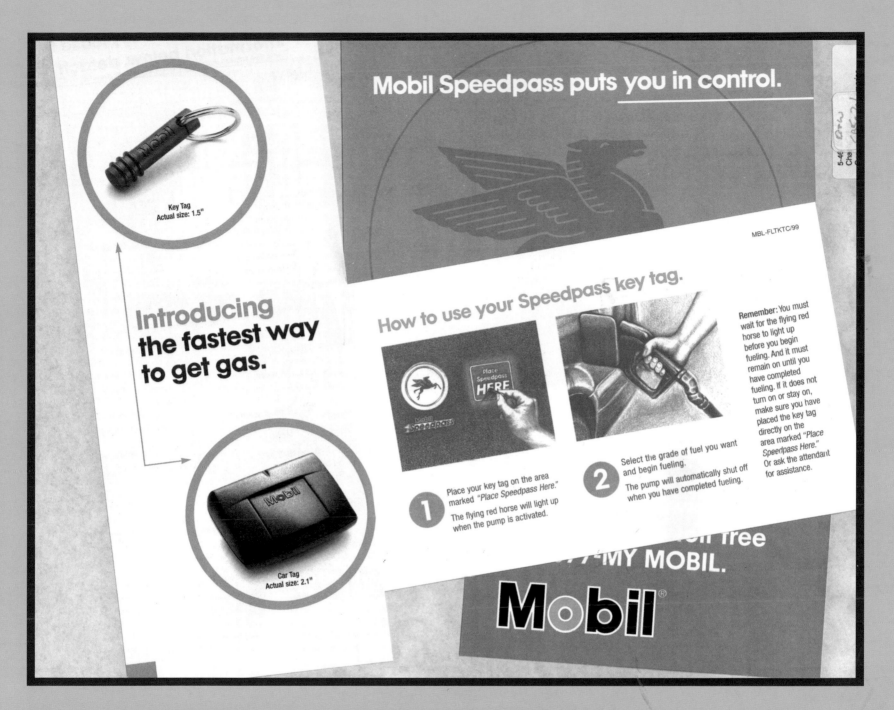

The Mobil SpeedPass is the best thing to happen to the gas station since the invention of the air hose. By using a keychain or car-mounted transponder, motorists may fill up their gas tank without having to bother with cash or a credit card. It's fast, easy, and makes stopping for gasoline a pleasure. *Courtesy Mobil Corporation*

Customers need not worry about having their new cars scratched up by the robot arm, either: Shell reports that over the three years of SmartPump testing, not one incident has been reported! There are a number of fail-safe systems in place as well, including one that automatically shuts down the system in the event of any sort of trouble. If the computer detects a problem it has not seen before, the whole system is disabled. For instance, if a customer pulled in and opened the car door or popped the hood, the motion detectors would sense a problem and shut down the system.

Energized by the success of the Shell system, many of the other oil companies are busy designing robotic gas pump systems of their own, including ExxonMobil. If technology continues at the same pace we are seeing today, it appears that the process of refueling a car will become completely automated by the year 2010—that is if automobiles are still running on gasoline!

With that said, what will the future hold for the gas and oil industry? The answers may surprise you,

American transportation is founded upon the notion of cheap and available gasoline. Hurray for the red, white, and blue! Let the gas pumps flow freely and put the pedal to the metal. ©2000 Coolstock.com

Soda pop signage can still be seen attached to the doors and walls of some country stores and shops. ©2000 Coolstock.com

Tow truck services used to be performed by the small-time operator. These days, it's a big-dollar business with fancy rigs that carry the entire car on a flatbed trailer. The tow truck of yesterday has become yet another relic. ©2000 Coolstock.com

The modern restroom is a ghost of what it once was. Today, motorists have a difficult time finding one off of the beaten path. When one is found, it is often necessary for the motorist to request a key, usually attached to a large object, in order to use the restroom. ©2000 Coolstock.com

as a myriad of alternate fuel, power sources, and vehicles that don't require gasoline are being developed by major players in the industry. Many have shown the potential to displace gas as a primary fuel source. The internal combustion engine, characterized by its harmful exhaust gases and noisy operation, may soon be replaced by clean running solar or hybrid vehicles. Goodbye to the gas station as we know it!

Toyota is turning heads with a splashy magazine advertising campaign and the slogan, "Ever heard the sound a stoplight makes?" It's all to introduce their latest breakthrough, a new hybrid car called the "Prius." It's the world's first car that combines a super-efficient gasoline engine with an electric motor that never needs to be plugged in. Seamlessly, the car switches between gas, electric, or a combination of both. It decides the

best way to power the car under a variety of driving conditions, and switches systems on and off on the fly. When the car stops at a traffic light, the engine stops! For a little over $20,000, prospective owners can save gasoline as they preserve the Earth's atmosphere.

Other car makers are waking up. Recently, the American Honda Motor Company furthered the cause of clean air when it introduced their own gas-electric vehicle. Dubbed the Honda "Insight," this new offering has gained recognition as the official pace car for 2000 Northeast Sustainable Energy Association (NESEA) American Tour de Sol road rally. Unlike America's first motoring events—which were staged to prove the extended capabilities of internal combustion gas engine, this rally focuses attention on alternative fuel sources. During a 250-mile course between New York City and Washington, D.C., cars, trucks, and buses will battle it out in an effort to determine the cleanest-running, most fuel-efficient vehicle in America. Movers and shakers in the industry are already taking notice: "The Honda Insight represents a superb application of advanced environmental technologies for everyday driving and we are happy to see it lead the 2000 NESEA American Tour de Sol," reports Nancy Hazard, associate director of

Arthur F. Bergeron, Peterborough, N. H.

Is it possible to travel the backroads and still find nostalgic scenes like this? According to reliable reports, this whimsical dealership, house, and gas station still exists. *Courtesy Coolstock.com*

Reptile Zoo and Gift Shop, Alton Bay, N. H.

On Lake Winnipesaukee

Travel the highways and byways of today and you will find that many of the roadside attractions of the 1950s and 1960s have disappeared. With the advent of large theme parks, vacationers don't often notice the small-time curiosities that may be found along the backroads. *Courtesy Coolstock.com*

This station on the outskirts of Texas hill country makes fine use of the native rock found in the region. They just don't make them like they used to! ©2000 Coolstock.com

The roadside gas station of simpler times has been recreated at this Salado, Texas, attraction right off of Interstate 35. ©2000 Coolstock.com

the NESEA. "With its ultra-high fuel economy and ultra-low emissions, the Honda Insight helps to conserve natural resources, reduce the impact on climate change and lower smog-forming emissions." You can bet the oil companies are watching!

No doubt, everyone will be at the event taking notes, as the Honda Insight vehicle epitomizes state of the art advancements in affordable environmental technology. As far as fuel efficiency is concerned, the Insight is capable of getting 70 miles to the gallon and approximately 61 miles per gallon in city traffic. Honda Motors estimates that for the Tour de Sol event, the pace car will need only four gallons of fuel for the entire run! With a 10.6 gallon capacity fuel tank, there won't be any stops made for gasoline!

The Insight is truly an affordable alternative to the monster trucks and sports utility gasoline hogs that currently dominate the highways. It's priced at less than $19,000, bringing it well below the average price of motor vehicles sold today. For their investment, environmentally-conscious car purchasers get

continued on page 171

On the outskirts of Wichita, Kansas, there is proof that the gas stations run by "mom and pop" can still survive, although it is a rare occurrence. Even though this image was taken at the dawn of the new millennium, it is greatly reminiscent of Farm Security Administration photographs taken during the 1930s. ©2000 Coolstock.com

The petroleum tankers are still rolling and the gasoline is still flowing freely in America. As we crank up our cars in the morning, we owe a great debt of thanks to the truckers. They are the people who bring it to market. ©2000 Coolstock.com

Various grades of gasoline and an integrated overhead canopy define today's gas pump experience. Cash is no longer needed as convenient debit card terminals allow consumers to use their credit cards and "pay at the pump." ©2000 Coolstock.com

Debit or credit? Today, the motorist has a choice when paying for gas at the pump. ©2000 Coolstock.com

Today, there is no gas station attendant at the gas pump with whom to chat. Electronic indicators and networked debit card readers comprise the brain of this new unit.
©2000 Coolstock.com

DESERT WATER BAGS

During the 1920s, motorists adventurous enough to make the journey across America were faced with many hardships. Gas stations were few and far in between. Repair facilities were a rare sight. In the great expanse between towns, the motorists had to rely on their own sense and ingenuity to complete their journies. That meant repairing flats along the way, carrying tools to do engine work, and toting along extra containers of oil and other fluids.

On top of this list was good old water. Not only was it a must for survival, the intrepid motorist had to have a supply on hand in case of a radiator boilover. One could run a car on the rims or limp along with a faulty clutch, but driving with an empty radiator was certain automotive suicide. To keep from cracking the head or seizing a cylinder, an engine had to have water circulating through it to maintain a cool equilibrium.

Of course, it didn't help that radiators of the era were delicate contrivances and underrated for the grueling conditions to which they were exposed. They overheated quickly in slow city traffic, and while chugging up steep hills during hot weather. Unperfected in their design, America's early radiators were prone to problems of the thermal kind, especially if the cooling fins were clogged with mud, grease, or plant matter. The science of thermodynamics was a long way from where we are today and many cars were designed poorly when it came to their cooling systems.

City dwellers who could afford a motoring compulsion had little to worry about, as they could easily find a fresh supply of water. The specter of radiator boilover loomed large when trips were made beyond the city limits, especially if that trip involved a region of the country where temperatures soared into the triple digits. During the summer, arid sections of Arizona's Route 66, as well as stretches of highway in California and Nevada, were notorious for bringing down even the finest cars.

"Last chance" filling stations that poised themselves on the edge of these domestic deserts had a booming business selling water! Signs warned motorists to fill up with fuel and to stock plenty of water. Billboards painted with the skull and crossbones reinforced the message; conjuring images of bleached cow skulls and stranded travelers crawling through the desert, dying of thirst. Remember, in that day and age, there was no air conditioning and ice cubes were considered a novelty.

To carry along their precious cache of water, motorists used the best technology available at the time. They used portable "water bags;" soft containers made of tightly woven Scotch flax or "genuine imported linen." After filling with water, canvas bags perspire with moisture as liquid oozes through special strands of cloth. The fibers allow the water to slowly leach through. When hung on the outside of a car window, over the hood ornament, or draped over the side-mount spare, the air rushing by creates a "wind chill" effect. Evaporation inside the pouch is what caused the water to remain cool—that is, as long as a car moved swiftly through the hot air in a forward motion.

For less than a dollar, the conscientious vehicle owner could purchase a water bag from any well-stocked filling station, auto repair garage, or general store. With all of the exposure that a water bag would get, it was a great form of advertising. On the exterior, manufacturers silkscreened all kinds of bold graphics to get people's attention. The Water Boy brand had a feathered Native American, the Hirsch Weis bag had a vaulting buck, and the Safari brand had a roaring lion.

W. A. Plummer's canvas bag featured the image of a pick and shovel along with the slogan, "Desert Water Bag."

Notwithstanding the graphics, water bags were generally manufactured exactly the same. They were rectangular with heavy border stitching and a removable cap. A length of string or chain secured the stopper so it wouldn't get lost. A few water bags tried to get fancy, and one or two used interesting gimmicks like a wooden hand-hold; however, most of them came with a heavy-duty carrying rope that was looped through eyelets and knotted at the two upper corners.

In spite of its utility, the glory days of the water bag were short lived. By the end of the 1950s, the necessity for carrying along a bulging bag of water was largely eliminated. New engine designs rendered the practice a moot point, as radiators were now more resistant to the elements. Keeping drinking water cool was an advancing science as well: Vacationers relied on insulated coolers and portable flasks such as those made by Thermos.

At long last, ice cubes were cranked out in large quantities by automatic ice makers at numerous gas stations, motels, and tourist attractions. To attract customers, filling stations across the land made "free ice water" a selling point! As America's traveling tourists raised a frigid flagon of icy drink to their lips, the water bags of motoring's early days were quickly forgotten.

173

pay a fee, or join a club that used a national debit card to debit their purchases.

At home, electric cars would be recharged by simply plugging a cable into a wall outlet or a curbside power port and waiting for the battery to return to its full capacity. It's likely that many consumers would invest in their own power generating solar cells to produce their own current. Either way, obtaining energy from the sun will be the most environmentally-friendly way to go since power obtained from the majority of conventional power plants is still produced by burning coal or other fuel. What's the point of operating a clean car if the main power plant still pollutes?

How does the American gas station play into all of this? As Bob Dylan sang in his memorable song, "The times they are a' changing." That change is most evident in the price of gasoline. As we enter the new millennium, fuel prices in America are skyrocketing to an all-time high. A few states are going so far as to relax the gas tax so consumers can still afford to travel! Delivery companies are adding fuel surcharges to their deliveries as the price of air, bus, and train travel spirals upward.

Meanwhile, giving the public inside information on where to obtain the cheapest gas has become a standard promotion for radio and TV stations. A radio station in San Antonio, Texas, recently held an on-air promotion where fuel at a local station was sold for the numerical amount of the station's broadcasting frequency, 96 FM. Z-102, another Texas station in Austin, has regular reports from "Petroleum Jerry," a masked avenger who roams the town looking for the cheapest places to gas up. Not only can you hear his reports over the radio airwaves, but you can call, fax, or e-mail!

So the next time you hit the road in search of fun and frolic, glance over to the side of the road and consider the gas station. Fill up your tank and take in the scene. As incredible as it might sound, the mini-market refueling stops of today will soon be as outmoded as the attendant-manned filling station of the 1920s!

Within a short time, the gas station will assume a completely different form and perform a completely different role. The most significant variable in this equation is that personal transportation is evolving at a breakneck pace. Whether we are prepared for it or not, a new age of service and a new range of features is coming soon to the gas stations across America!

The sun is setting on the institution known as the American gas station. In the near future, expect more change than ever before. ©2000 Coolstock.com

Bibliography

Anderson, Scott. *Check the Oil: Gas Station Collectibles with Prices.* Pittsburgh, PA: Wallace-Homestead Book Co., 1986.

Anderson, Warren H. *Vanishing Roadside America.* Tucson, AZ: The University of Arizona Press, 1981.

Anderson, Will. *Mid-Atlantic Roadside Delights.* Portland, ME: Anderson & Sons Publishing Co., 1991.

Anderson, Will. *New England Roadside Delights.* Portland, ME: Anderson & Sons Publishing Co., 1989.

Baeder, John. *Gas, Food, and Lodging: A Postcard Odyssey Through the Great American Roadside.* New York: Abbeville Press, 1982.

"Baker Oil Company Presents Extensive New Calsteel Built Service Facility." *Gas Station and Garage* 34 (May 1950): 10.

Bayer, Patricia. *Art Deco Sourcebook.* Secaucus, NJ: The Wellfleet Press, 1988.

Beaton, Kendall. *Enterprise in Oil.* New York: Appleton-Century-Crofts, Inc., 1957.

Bogstahl, Mars. "Storm Warnings Up For Stations." *National Petroleum News* 56 (July 1964): 103–106.

Boyne, Walter J. *Power Behind the Wheel: Creativity and Evolution of the Automobile.* New York: Stewart, Tabori & Chang, 1988.

A Brief History of Mobil. Fairfax, VA: Mobil Corporation, 1991.

"By-Pass Highways for Traffic Relief." *American City* 38 (April 1928): 88–90.

"Calcor Built Neighborhood Station Features Complete Service For Every Car." *Gas Station and Garage* 34 (February 1950): 8.

"Canopies: What's Behind an Old Standby's New Appeal." *National Petroleum News* 50 (November 1958): 99–104.

Chaffee, Wib. "What is a 'Super Service' Station?" *Automobile Digest* (February 1929): 12–13, 68–70.

"Changes at the Pump." *Time* 86 (9 July 1965): 90.

Coate, Roland E. "An Auto Service Station." *Architectural Record* 63 (April 1928): 303.

Crosser, C.A. "Curbing the Curb Pump." *American City* 29 (August 1923): 155–156.

Dale, Crag. "Is Main Street Doomed?" *Popular Mechanics* 55 (May 1931): 756–768.

"A Detour for Roadside America." *Business Week* (16 February 1974): 44.

"Does Beauty Sell? Mobil Tries to Find Out." *National Petroleum News* 58 (November 1966):120.

"Down They Come." *Standard Oil Bulletin* 11 (March 1924): 3.

Draper, George O. "A View of the Tour from One Participating." *Horseless Age* 16 (26 July 1905): 153.

Edmond, Mark. "What Marketers Are Doing or Not Doing About Closed Stations." *National Petroleum News* 64 (April 1972): 82–85.

"Elevating the Standing of the 'Hot Dog Kennel.'" *American City* 38 (May 1928): 99–100.

Elwell, Richard R. "California is Off Again, As . . . Multipumps Revive the Canopy." *National Petroleum News* 47 (November 1955): 41–42.

"Filling Stations as Embryo Cities." *Literary Digest* 107 (29 November 1930): 44.

Flink, James J. *The Automobile Age.* Cambridge, MA: The M.I.T. Press, 1988.

Frazer, Elizabeth. "The Destruction of Rural America: Game, Fish and Flower Hogs." *The Saturday Evening Post* (9 May 1929): 39, 193–194, 197–198.

"'Gas-A-Terias': Self-Served Gasoline Saves a Nickel a Gallon for California Drivers." *Life* 25 (22 November 1948): 129.

"Gasoline: Help Yourself Boom." *Newsweek* 30 (29 December 1947): 48.

"Gasoline: War Against Self-Service." *Newsweek* 33 (25 April 1949): 69–70.

Gasoline Pump Blue Book. New York: Gasoline Pump Manufacturers Association, 1952.

"Gasoline Stations Become Architectural Assets." *American City* 41 (November 1929): 98–99.

Gelderman, Carol. *Henry Ford: The Wayward Capitalist.* New York: St. Martin's Press, 1981.

Hastings, Charles Warren. "Roadtown, The Linear City." *Architects and Builders Magazine* 10 (August 1910): 445.

Heat Moon, William Least. *Blue Highways: A Journey Into America.* Boston: Atlantic Monthly Press, 1982.

Helen Christine Bennett, "'Pinkie's Pantry' Took The Cake." *American Magazine* (June 1928): 65–66.

Hocke, John. "An Up-to-Date Greasing Palace." *American Builder and Building Age* 52 (December 1930): 80–81.

Hokansen, Drake. *The Lincoln Highway: Main Street Across America.* Iowa City: University of Iowa Press, 1988.

"How Ranch Style is Taking Over Service-Station Design." *National Petroleum News* 58 (May 1966): 95–101.

Hungerford, Edward. "America Awheel." *Everybody's Magazine* 36 (June 1917): 678.

Jakle, John A. "The American Gasoline Station, 1920–1970." *Journal of American Culture* 1 (Spring 1978): 520–542.

James, Marquis. *The Texaco Story: The First Fifty Years 1902–1952.* New York: The Texas Company, 1953.

Jones, Charles L. *Service Station Management: Its Principles and Practice.* New York: D. Van Nostrand Company, 1922.

Jordan, Michael. "Lost in the Fifties." *Automobile Magazine* (November 1988): 123–125.

Keller, Ulrich. *The Highway as Habitat: A Roy Stryker Documentation, 1943–1955.* Santa Barbara, CA: University Art Museum, 1986.

Kerouac, Jack. *On the Road.* New York: Viking Penguin, 1955.

Knowles, Ruth Sheldon. *The First Pictorial History of the American Oil and Gas Industry 1859–1983.* Athens, OH: Ohio University Press, 1983.

Kowinski, William Severini. "Suburbia: End of the Golden Age." *The New York Times Magazine* (16 March 1980): 16–19, 106.

Kuntz, J.F. "Greek Architecture and Gasoline Service Stations." *American City* 27 (August 1922): 123–124.

Langdon, Philip. *Orange Roofs, Golden Arches: The Architecture of American Chain Restaurants.* New York: Alfred A. Knopf, 1986.

Lay, Charles Downing. "New Towns for High-Speed Roads." *Architectural Record* 78 (November 1935): 352–354.

Lee, Bob. *Tokheim Pump Company: An Illustrated History.* Detroit, MI: Harlo Press, 1980.

Liebs, Chester. *Main Street to Miracle Mile: American Roadside Architecture.* Boston: Little, Brown & Co., 1985.

"Life After Death Along Gasoline Alley." *Fortune* (5 November 1979): 86–89.

Link, Joe. "Attacks on Service Stations Mount While Oil Remains Silent." *National Petroleum News* 64 (March 1972): 46–48.

Lohof, Bruce A. "The Service Station in America: The Evolution of a Vernacular Form." *Industrial Archeology* 11 (1974): 1–13.

Londberg-Holm, K. "The Gasoline Filling and Service Station." *Architectural Record* 67 (June 1930) 563–571.

Love, Ed. *Gas and Oil Trademarks: Volume 2.* Colorado Springs: Villa Publishing Syndicate, 1990.

Love, Ed. *United States Design Patents: Series 1.* Colorado Springs: Villa Publishing Syndicate, 1990.

Love, Ed, and Larry T. Drivas. *Gas and Oil Trademarks: Volume 1.* Colorado Springs: Villa Publishing Syndicate, 1988.

Lowe, Lucy. "Service Stations as an Asset to the City." *American City* 25 (August 1921): 151–153.

Mackaye, Benton, and Lewis Mumford. "Townless Highways for the Motorist." *Harper's* 163 (August 1931): 347–356.

Margolies, John. *The End of the Road: Vanishing Highway Architecture in America.* New York: The Viking Press, 1981.

Marling, Karal Ann. *The Colossus of Roads: Myth and Symbol Along the American Highway.* Minneapolis: University of Minnesota Press, 1984.

McCabe, Axe, and Ed Love. *Gas Stations and Related Designs: Volume 1.* Colorado Springs: Villa Publishing Syndicate, 1989.

McCabe, Axe, and Ed Love. *Gas Stations and Related Designs: Volume 3.* Colorado Springs: Villa Publishing Syndicate, 1990.

Mills, Joseph E. *Garage Management and Control.* New York: A.W. Shaw Company, 1928.

Minnick, Richard G. "The Silent Sentinel of the American Road Part One." *Antique Automobile* (January 1964): 17–27.

"Money to be Made: The Oil Marketing Story." *National Petroleum News* 61 (February 1969): 111–130.

Moore, Stanley T. "Individual Service Station Design." *National Petroleum News* 25 (14 June 1933): 53–57.

"Motorists Tell in Their Own Words What They Expect at Filling Stations." *National Petroleum News* (17 November 1926): 92.

National Trust for Historic Preservation. *Ducks & Diners.* Edited by Diane Maddex and Janet Walker, Washington, D.C.: The Preservation Press, 1988.

"New Life for Old Stations." *National Petroleum News* 56 (September 1964): 101–104.

Oppel, Frank. *Motoring in America: The Early Years.* Secaucus, NJ: Castle Books, 1989.

Partridge, Bellamy. *Fill 'er Up!* Reprint. Los Angeles: Floyd Clymer, 1959.

Patton, Phil. *Open Road: A Celebration of the American Highway.* New York: Simon & Schuster, 1986.

Phillips Petroleum Co. *Phillips: The First 66 Years.* Edited by William C. Wertz. A public affairs publication of Phillips Petroleum Co., 1983.

Phillips Petroleum Co. *Why 66?* Bartlesville, OK: 1991.

Platt, Warren C. "Competition Invited by the Nature of the Oil Industry." *National Petroleum News* (5 February 1936): 205.

"Prototype for Service Stations: Mobil Tests Effect of Design on Sales at 58 Locations." *Architectural Record* 141 (May 1967): 172–175.

"Prototype Gas Station Looks Like a Winner—And Is." *Progressive Architecture* 53 (October 1972): 31.

"Pump's Progress: The Tower to Match the Power." *Texaco Dealer* (February 1958): 8–10.

Reid, Marvin. "The Sophisticated Self-Serve Comes of Age, Part I: Self-Serves and C-Stores." *National Petroleum News* 69 (July 1977): 54–63.

Ridder, Holger. "Stations Become Merchandising Tools for Boosting Sales, Giving Better Service." *National Petroleum News* (29 March 1950): 26–40.

Ripp, Bart. "All Pumped Up." *Tacoma News Tribune* (25 July 1989).

Rowsome, Frank Jr. *The Verse by the Side of the Road.* MA: Stephen Greene Press, 1965.

"Scenic or Sign-ic?" *Standard Oil Bulletin* 17 (September 1929): 14–16.

Schroeder, Richard C. "How and When to Modernize Your Service Stations." *National Petroleum News* 50 (October 1958): 84–89.

Scott, Quinta. *Route 66: The Highway and its People*. Norman, OK: The University of Oklahoma Press, 1988.

Sculle, Keith A. "C.A. Petersen: Pioneer Gas Station Architect." *Historic Illinois* 2 (June 1979): 11–13.

Sculle, Keith A. "The Vernacular Gasoline Station: Examples From Illinois and Wisconsin." *Journal of Cultural Geography* 1 (Spring-Summer 1981): 56–74.

"Self-Service Moves in on the Pump." *Business Week* (1 October 1966): 129–130.

"Self-Service Stations: New Marketing Pattern?" *Business Week* (24 July 1948): 68.

"Service-Station Beautification is Coming in for Ever-Increasing Attention." *National Petroleum News* 58 (March 1966): 81–82.

"Service-Station Design." *National Petroleum News* 42 (29 March 1950): 30.

"Service Stations." *Architectural Record* 97 (February 1944): 71–92.

"Service Stations: The Needless Blot." *Fortune* 74 (September 1966): 159–160.

"Shell Oil's Newest 'Blend-In.'" *National Petroleum News* 52 (February 1960): 121.

Silk, Gerald, Angelo Anselmi, Henry Robert, Jr., and Strother MacMinn. *Automobile and Culture*. New York: Harry N. Abrams, Inc., 1984.

Sinclair Oil Corporation. *A Great Name in Oil: Sinclair Through Fifty Years*. Editorial consultant, Hartzell Spence. F.W. Dodge Co./McGraw-Hill, Inc., 1966.

Society for Commercial Archeology. *The Automobile in Design and Culture*. Edited by Jan Jennings. Ames: Iowa State University Press, 1990.

Squire, Latham C., and Howard M. Bassett. "A New Type of Thoroughfare: The 'Freeway.'" *American City* 47 (November 1932): 64–66.

"Staebler Opens Modern Station in Ann Arbor." *National Petroleum News* 25 (31 May 1933): 34.

"Standardized Service Stations Designed by Walter Dorwin Teague." *Architectural Record* 82 (September 1937): 69–72.

Steinbeck, John. *The Grapes of Wrath*. New York: The Viking Press, 1939.

Steinbeck, John. *Travels with Charley*. New York: The Viking Press, 1962.

Stern, Jane, and Michael Stern. *Road Food*. New York: Random House, 1980.

Stern, Rudi. *Let There Be Neon*. New York: Harry N. Abrams, Inc., 1979.

"Super Service Station: A Plan for a Corner Lot." *Automobile Digest* 17 (January 1929): 37.

Sweeney, Don. "California's Self Service Stations Still in Limelight." *National Petroleum News* 40 (25 May 1948): 9.

Sweeney, Don. "New Stations Designed to Stress Eye Appeal in Pushing the Sale of TBA." *National Petroleum News* 40 (14 January 1948): 36–37.

Teague, Walter Dorwin. *Design This Day: The Technique of Order in the Machine Age*. New York: Harcourt, Brace & Co., 1940.

Thomas, Diane C. "Lonely Road Now." *Atlanta Magazine* (November 1978): 57–59, 123–124.

Thompson, Craig. *Since Spindletop: A Human Story of Gulf's First Half-Century*. Pittsburgh, PA: Gulf Oil Corporation, 1951.

"Tokheim Corporation: Poised for a Gas Pump Boom." *Dun's Review* (October 1979): 20–25.

"Tomorrow's Gas Station." *Popular Science* 149 (November 1946): 100–101.

"Travel Service With a Twist." *National Petroleum News* 52 (February 1960): 118.

"Treads and Threads." *Time* (12 October 1981): 72.

"Vacancies on Gasoline Alley." *Business Week* (15 December 1953): 20–21.

Veeder-Root, Inc. *20 Years of Development*. CT: 1991.

Vieyra, Daniel I. *Fill 'er Up: An Architectural History of America's Gas Stations*. New York: Collier MacMillan Publishers Inc., 1979.

Von Eckardt, Wolf. "Toward a Better Community: Must Gas Stations Be Garish?" *American Home* (June 1967): 40–41.

Wallis, Michael. *Route 66: The Mother Road*. New York: St. Martin's Press, 1990.

Walton, Richard J. *The Power of Oil*. New York: The Seabury Press, 1977.

"Wayside Stands, Billboards, Curb Pumps, Lunch Wagons, Junk Yards, and Their Ilk." *American City* 44 (April 1931): 104–108.

"Who'll Get Helped or Hurt by Auto Freeways." *U.S. News and World Report* (21 December 1956): 90–92.

Wilson, Richard Guy, Dianne H. Pilgrim, and Dickran Tashjian. *The Machine Age in America 1918–1941*. New York: Harry N. Abrams, Inc., 1986.

Witzel, Michael. *The American Gas Station*. Osceola, WI: MBI Publishing Company, 1992.

Witzel, Michael. *Gas Station Memories*. Osceola, WI: MBI Publishing Company, 1994.

Woodson, LeRoy. *Roadside Food*. New York: Stewart, Tabori & Chang, Inc., 1986.

Index